PICTORIAL DISTRIBUTION
OF REGIONAL DANCES OF SPAIN

SPANISH DANCING

Other Works by

LA MERI

THE DANCE

Principles of the Dance-Art
CHANNING-RENTON, Paris, 1931

Dance as an Art-Form
A. S. BARNES & COMPANY, New York, 1935

Gesture Language of the Hindu Dance
COLUMBIA UNIVERSITY PRESS, New York, 1942

POETRY

Mexican Moonlight
CORNWALL PRESS, Boston, 1922

Poems of the Plains
RICHARD BADGER, Boston, 1922

The Star Roper
DORRANCE AND CO., Philadelphia, 1924

The Star Roper (special edition)
SUNSET PRESS, New York, 1928

Songs and Voyages
PRIVATELY PRINTED, Leghorn, 1938

SPANISH DANCING

BY

LA MERI

A. S. BARNES & COMPANY, New York

DEDICATION

To another enthusiastic exponent of the
Spanish dance, my beloved sister LILIAN.

AUTHOR'S NOTE

This book has been long in the making. It was begun with the gathering of material on my very first trip to Spain. It is not finished nor can it ever be, for it seeks to describe an art and only an art that is dead ceases to change with growth and expansion. These pages are offered, with some diffidence, in the hope that they will inspire others to add to the somewhat meager published works on Spanish dancing.

I wish to thank, with a full heart, all the great Spanish dancers who have lifted me outside time and space with their inimitable artistry. I wish to thank Juan Martinez, José Otero, Pilar Lopez, Murcillo Laborda, La Bisca, Carmen de Toledo and all those others who have patiently answered my numberless questions. And in the final preparation of this book, let me also thank Juana, Edna Dieman and Pietro di Falco, for their practical assistance.

CONTENTS

FOREWORD

It has been La Meri's purpose, both as performing artist and teacher, to bring the world's dances to the attention of the American public. Her authentic re-creations of ethnologic dance forms have afforded the beholder opportunities to enjoy aspects of dance new to him, to become partially familiar with the customs of alien peoples through the patterns of dance and, perhaps, to learn something of the nature of his fellow men in pleasant and painless fashion. In order to carry out this purpose, she traveled the world in search of dance and has mastered the forms she desired to carry back to her native shores. To do the task correctly, it was necessary for her to do more than learn the physical outlines of a given dance. She had to seek out the spirit behind it, the tradition it bore, the heritage from which it was derived, and this research she accomplished with the qualities of scholarliness and adventure.

In this book on Spanish dancing, La Meri provides the reader with the results of her adventure into and experience with the dances of Spain. Much of the value of this book lies, strangely enough, in the fact that La Meri is not a Spaniard; yet she is, of course, a recognized authority on Spanish dancing. As an American, she is able to view Spanish dancing objectively, to translate its purposes and qualities into American terms for the benefit of her uninitiated compatriots, and because of her long association with Spanish dance, she can make such translations accurately.

Her book, I think, has a three-fold purpose: to assist the general reader in quickening and deepening his interest in Spanish dance by taking him to the cities and towns and cafes where the dances were born and by describing them in vivid detail; to assist the student of dance by providing him with rules of technique and of style and by giving him the necessary historical material without which his under-

standing of Spanish dance would be incomplete; to contribute to
Spanish dance itself by offering a generous glossary of technical
terms, the beginnings of a Spanish dance dictionary. This final section will undoubtedly prove to be a controversial one, for even
among Spanish dancers there are disagreements on the meanings of
many technical terms; however, a standardization of technical terminology is certainly desirable, particularly for teaching purposes
and La Meri is to be congratulated for her willingness to venture
into a battle area. Whether it is upon safe ground or dangerous
ground, whether it is reporting or exploring, La Meri's newest book
constitutes an important and pleasurable adventure into the realm of
Spanish dance.

WALTER TERRY

SPANISH DANCING

PANADEROS—LA MERI

Chapter

I

INTRODUCTION

What can I say of the Spanish dance? Great writers since Pliny have set down immortal phrases describing its fire and verve and perennial charm. Yet who can reflect in the immutable phrase, the heart-lift in watching emotion in motion? Like quicksilver it slips through the hands, the very facts grow confused and unreliable. Spanish dancers themselves disagree and delve into the past to bring to light disheartening contradictions.

And yet, perhaps, there is still something to be added—something to be clarified.

We have been told since we first heard a castanet click, that only Spaniards could dance Spanish. It is a theory upon which, in this fine, free country, each may have his own opinion. But there are, to my personal knowledge, exceptions—there was a great teacher of Spanish dancers who was not Spanish; there are great Spanish dancers, male and female, who are not Spanish; there are dancers who have passed for Spanish among Spaniards.

The Spanish dance has enjoyed a popularity unequalled by any other dance-form. Since Carthage it has fascinated the world. Today it is known and loved everywhere. Every little dancing school in the United States presents, in its yearly recital, a local maiden equipped with castanets and comb. In India the Hindus applaud the Spanish dance mightily.

In the night clubs of all the world, from Paris to Singapore, the Spanish dance is a favorite in the floor show; and afterwards, its influence shadows provocatively in rumba and tango. From Petipa to Massine, ballet choreographers have worked in the Spanish medium; and Argentinita, with her ensemble, was the best box-office attraction in the concert dance field in this decade.

S. L. M. Barlow [1] writes that "there are perhaps three schools of dancing; the Indian, the Russian (which for the moment commands ideas essentially Italian or French) and the Modern, which includes Graham, Wigman, Weidman and several junior groups, here in Europe." [2] I would venture to add that the Spanish, which does not stem from any of the three, in its Flamenco form, bears as much resemblance to the Indian, as to the Russian.

Many "estranjeros" (foreigners) make the mistake of believing that the Spanish dance can be learned "on the side,"—a useful adjunct to ballet, or tap, or whatever. Without digressing into a discussion of how many types of dancing any one performer can get away with, it would be well to try to make the point in this book that Spanish dancing has a complete technique and many facets within its own style. It is no more a folk dance. As I see it, the difference in a folk dance and a dance-art being this: a folk dance is without a basic technique—can be danced by anyone with rhythm and desire; the style itself being a very unimportant part of the essential scope of the dance—whether that dance be of the United States, India, Norway or Chile. A dance-art has a definite basic technique, and one which must be mastered before the dance is approached. The style is the very essence of the dance itself— ballet, Javanese, Japanese, Spanish and such types.

Since earliest occidental history the Spanish dance has been the richest, the most variated, and the most highly developed of all western national dances. "So thorough is its fundamental nobility and so finished its technique that many exponents of the Italian ballet concede to it superiority over all in that aspect of beauty which is concerned with majesty of line and posture." [3]

There are forty-nine provinces in Spain, the whole country one-thirtieth the size of the United States, and yet there exist over a hundred accepted, unchangeable, traditional dances.

The enthusiastic Charbonnel [4] writes, "The Spaniard not only loves the dance, it is for him a cult. The dance is a part of his heart, like his sun, his country and his dreams. They say if you deprive a Spaniard of

---

[1] S. L. M. Barlow, in an article in Modern Music—March-April 1944.

[2] Martha Graham and Charles Weidman (American), Mary Wigman (German); contemporary.

[3] Kinney, Troy and Margaret West, "The Dance," Frederick Stokes, 1914, New York.

[4] Raoul Charbonnel, "La Danse," Garnier Frères, 1899, Paris.

his 'chocolate a la canela' he will sicken, but if you deprive him of the dance he will die!" That other French historian of the dance, Vuillier, writes, "Spain is today as Greece once was, the classic land of the dance." [5] Not only do they dance in processions, as all know, and around the honored dead, but in pilgrimages, in village fêtes, on the roads that lead to the fairs. They dance without reason and anywhere for pleasure. Their holidays are spent, cigarette between lips, waiting for the "corrida" (bullfight) and contemplating the "zapateado." [6] The dark "gitana" (gypsy) of ardent eyes and white teeth, rattles her "panadero" (tambourine) in the square and on roads, or even on the tables of a "fonda" (café) before a chance public. The Spanish dances are original, expressive, variated and charming above all others. The dancers have grace, pride, dash and passion joined with an incomparable "souplesse."

It is the strange mixture of East and West which gives the Spanish dance its allure. For nothing excites us so much as that which we can never quite understand or that which we may love but never possess. Its very elusiveness makes its earthiness more sensual. The western dance smiles, opens outward, both physically and spiritually, leaps and expresses its sentiments for all to see. Its "joie de vivre" is uncontained and contagious. The oriental dance is serious, nearly sad, it closes on itself, pondering on another world; it is calm and without climax; it keeps its sentiments controlled and deeply hidden. But the Spanish dance partakes of both these elements, and so is as changeable as spring.

"It is no accomplishment for a Spaniard to be able to dance, to be able to sing. Everybody dances. Everybody sings." [7] And for this reason "half the graceful dancing of the world has come from Spain." [8]

Perhaps this very spontaneity, this very universalness of the knowledge of the dance is the reason why the Spaniard so seldom approaches the art from a purely choreographic view. And the foreigner, starting out with the avowed intention of clarifying the rules, solidifying the dynamic and plastic character, discovering the source of its form, suddenly finds he has flung away notebook and pencil, has joined in the "jaleo," [9] and is improvising couplets like any "flamenco" (gypsy). It is a dance which makes poets of us all.

Here we speak of Iberian dancers who have come to our shores; or, whose shadows have touched us from Paris and London. Hermetic Spain is that promised land to which we go to find within its borders

[5] Gaston Vuillier, "La Danse," Hachette & Co., 1898, Paris.
[6] Zapateado—dance (strictly speaking, rhythmic pattern of beaten foot).
[7] Charles Isaacson, in an article in The Dance Magazine (ca. 1925).
[8] Paul Morand, "Spring in Spain," Vogue Magazine, 1931.
[9] See Glossary of Terms.

the greatest—and the worst—Spanish dancing in the world. Many are the immortal artists who have flourished on the Peninsula, their names and careers unknown outside its borders. Few are the flowers that have braved the spiritual change of climate of going abroad. Let us dedicate this book to those courageous dancers, who, leaving their hearts in Spain, have brought the Spanish dance to us.

Chapter

II

HISTORY

*T*he earliest known visitors to Iberia were the Phoenicians (1600 B.C.). Historians have left us no words of the choreography of that period, but there are folk dances in Spain today which are said to be derived from the Phoenicians.

With the Hellenic supremacy in the Mediterranean (550 B.C.), we can begin to trace origins and influences in the dance. Castanets, now exclusively Spanish, were used in Greek dancing, as we can see from vases and figurines still existing. The counter-line in the arms, the arched back and head, the spiral movements, all so characteristic of Spanish choreography, were also present in the Greek, as was the participation of the spectators by rhythmically clapping the hands (jaleo). The Sardana of Catalunya is said to proceed from the Pyrrhic dance, as are many other communal dances of Spain; and, to derive from a still more primitive cult of sun worshipers, the choreography suggesting the passing of that life-giving orb. The contemporary Sirtos is very similar to the Sardana, as are the Hungarian Czardas and Rumanian Sarba, and its music has retained for twenty centuries the Mixolydian mode. There is a Homeric poem in the "Iliad" which describes a dance done by girls which is similar to the Sardana and the Muiñeira.

Other writers claim Egypt to be the mother of Spanish dancing. Martial coupled Gaditanian song-dances with those of the Nile. Certainly, there are myriad signs of the kinship between the gypsy dance and the Egyptian, but most historians believe this influence to have arrived in Spain with the Moorish Caliphates, and the gypsies, not

5

Photo by Philcox

EDNA DIEMAN in "Telathusa"

the Spaniard, to be the "sons and daughters of Pharaoh." Chase writes that "the first gypsies arrived in Spain as late as 1449." [1] Inzenga y Castellanos likens the dances of Valencia to those performed by the Egyptians during funeral ceremonies, while the Zortzico Vasconado seems an imitation of Egyptian sacred dances and Hebrew "saltaciones." "The cymbal, the tambourine, triangles, castanets, in one form or another, were all familiar to the ancient Egyptians and with the Egyptian art of dancing they must have spread all around the shores of the Mediterranean the great focus of our civilization at a very early date. Even beyond the Mediterranean, at Cadiz, dancing that was essentially Egyptian in character was established, and Cadiz became the dancing school of Spain. The Nile and Cadiz were thus the two great centers of ancient dancing and Martial mentions them both together, for each supplied its dancers to Rome." [2]

Certainly, the eastern and southern provinces of the Peninsula have been the recipient, each in its turn, of the cultural influences of the highest western civilizations. What emerges most strongly in the study of the ancient history of the Spanish dance is that 2000 years ago Spain was the dancing nation of the occident and that title she has not yet ceded to any people.

Cadiz (then called Gadir) was a center of art and culture when Carthage ruled the western world, and when Rome was the mastering occidental empire, "las Andaluces delicias" were the dancers most adored by both artistic and social circles. In fact their popularity was so great that the aristocratic ladies of Rome launched a mode for wearing earrings and necklaces fashioned like tiny "chinchines" (crotals) and castanets. The greatest among the Roman poets, Pliny, Silius Italicus, Petrone, Strabo and others, left to us enthusiastic strofes dedicated to these charming artists, and it was Telathusa, the "gaditana," celebrated in the epigrams of Martial, who served as model for the famous statue of "Venus Callipyge."

Between 476 and 711 A.D., Spain was overrun by the Visigoths. Toledo was then the capital and was, with Saragossa and Sevilla, the center of culture and activity. But little is known of the art of this period and we must wait for the coming of the Moors for information on the dance.

The invasion of the Moors drove many Spaniards into the north. Of all Spain only Galicia, Asturia, and part of Navarra and of Leon never came under Moorish domination, although something of oriental culture penetrated even there.

[1] Gilbert Chase, "The Music of Spain," W. W. Norton & Co., Inc., N. Y., 1941.
[2] Havelock Ellis, "The Soul of Spain," Houghton Mifflin Co., 1909, London.

During the Caliphate of Cordoba (912-961) dance and music performances under patronage were frequent if not nightly. Song and dance carried the same title and we find already the Zarabanda, the Sorongo and the Zambra appearing. The Zambra was a couple dance, being often still danced as such, and is a product of the Andalucian Moors. The Sorongo appeared, together with the Zarabanda, at the "leilas" which was the name given to the song-and-dance festivals.

The Zarabanda seems to have passed through an amazing evolution. First definitely heard of in 1589 in "Cancionero Clasico," a collection of dance-songs, it is still suspected of Near Eastern origin of an even earlier date. The reason for ascribing its birth to the Orient is partly etymological and partly because it was "so indecent in its movements, that even the most respectable people were inflamed by it." [3] The Zarabanda was danced at the Feast of Corpus Christi in Seville in 1593, and in spite of the fact that a law was passed (1583) punishing with two hundred lashes the singing of the coplas, it continued to appear from time to time in the Autos Sacramentales. Although exact choreography is missing, many contemporary authorities, deeply shocked by performances of the Zarabanda, have left us general descriptions of this "obscene" dance. However, by 1618 it had undergone a transformation so complete that it was taken into the formal gatherings of the somber Spanish court of the Inquisition!

With the fall of Granada (1492) and the accession of "los Reyes Catolicos" began a renaissance, and foremost among the protected arts was the dance. During this period Juan del Encina [4] inaugurated the Spanish drama with his pastoral playlets called "Eclogues" concluding each with a "villancico" which used dancing. Del Encina's Portuguese contemporary, Gil Vicente, writing in Spanish, first used the dance-song "folio." Soon masques and fiestas became the vogue and from Spain came many of the court dances which were popular all over Europe: the Pavane which imitates the movement of a peacock with such dignity that some have been dedicated to the Virgin Mary; the Pasacalle, which was often sung at leilas under the Caliphate, and which certain authorities believe, soon became the Passepied; the Chacona, (which Fernandez de Cordova claims is an ancient Cadiz dance called "Olé Gaditane") and the Zarabanda.

Curt Sachs writes "the sarabande and chaconne are truly exotic dances. They originated in the melting pot of Central America, were brought home to Andalucia by the colonists, stripped of their cruder suggestions on Spanish soil, polished, painfully adapted to European

[3] Juan di Mariana, 1536-1623.
[4] Juan del Encina—composer, end of 15th and beginning of 16th centuries.

non-imitativeness and close movement, and in this transformation introduced into the courtly dance north of the Pyrenees." [5]

Philip IV of Spain, like Louis XIV of France, became so enamored of the dance that he brought it to the theater. It was in 1657 that Calderon de la Barca wrote, "El Golfo de las Sirenas," a production using song, dance and dialogue. Presented at the Palace of the Zarzuela (a hunting lodge of the king) the form soon became popular and is still known in Spain as the Zarzuela. These musical comedy pieces were often followed by an "act" of dancing unrelated to the piece, and called "fin de fiesta." The fin de fiesta also persists in popularity today.

The dance was an amusement for the aristocracy, and as such, dignity was the keynote. The king himself danced in court and theater and it was natural that the choreography around him was of a restrained type. But there soon appeared a mode for the pastoral. The court took to giving fiestas in the fields and woods. It followed that the peasant dances were seen and admired by these elegant ladies and gentlemen, and straightway a new type of choreography came into being. At the Escurial, court ladies covered their powdered hair with the popular mantilla and danced the Fandango and Bolero.

Padre Pierre Martin writing in 1712, declared that the Fandango was celebrated in Cadiz for many centuries; it might indeed have descended from the repertoire of "las Andaluces delicias," for the Phoenicians themselves are said to have aided in its formation. The Fandango is a couple dance, from it stemmed the Malagueña, the Granadina, the Murciana, and the Rondeña, changing little in the environments from which it took its new names. Some authorities say it dates from 1000 and that in its courtly form it became the minuet. "The rhythm of the Fandango is a psychological phenomenon, catching at the throat and whipping the nerves." [6]

Baron Davillier [7] tells of this famous dance an incident, the authenticity of which I leave in the hands of that admirable writer. It seems that official Rome, scandalized at the Fandango and its hold on the people, decided that the performance of this dance would merit excommunication. A court was held and the Fandango was found guilty. But a certain cardinal present suggested that it was unfair to

---

[5] Curt Sachs, "World History of the Dance," W. W. Norton & Co., Inc., 1937, New York.

[6] André Levinson, "Argentina," Editions des Chroniques du Jour, 1928, Paris.

[7] Baron Davillier—"Une ancedote singulière dont nous ne voulons pas garantir l'authenticité, dit le baron Davillier, est racontée par un auteur du siècle dernier au sujet de cette danse fameuse." Gaston Vuillier, "La Danse," Chap. IX p. 286, Hachette and Co., 1898, Paris.

Comienzos del siglo XIX. — Fandango

(Litografía francesa)

Courtesy A. Martin, Barcelona

FANDANGO—a lithograph

The picture suggests a rustic picnic in a romantic landscape. Food and Spanish wine having heightened the gaiety of the group, a young girl begins to dance the Fandango to the rhythmic beats of her castañuelas and the accompaniment of instruments and hand clapping of her companions.

judge the subject without letting it speak for itself. Admitting the justice of this, the court sent for two dancers, man and woman, who danced before the august assembly the joyous Fandango. At the first measure clerical frowns disappeared and soon here and there wide robes moved as the foot beneath began to mark the heart-raising tempo. Soon the good fathers were clapping their hands and urging the dancers to even more brilliant steps. With the last "golpe des pieds" (stamp of the feet), his Eminence sank back exhausted in his chair and the Fandango was re-established in all honor. "From the narratives of travelers, it would appear that it was especially in the 18th century that among all classes in Spain dancing of this kind was popular. The church tacitly encouraged it, an Aragonese Canon told Baretti in 1770, in spite of its occasional indecorum, as a useful safety-valve for the emotions . . . and, even that highly respectable Anglican clergyman, the Reverend Joseph Townsend, was constrained to state that he could 'almost persuade myself' that if the Fandango were suddenly played in church, the gravest worshipers would start up to join in that lascivious pantomime." [8]

A few years after the Fandango inflamed the nation, the Bolero appeared. The name "Bolero" is taken from the Spanish word "volar" (fly). Dr. Sachs writes, "the bolero also depicts the woman slipping away, approaching and escaping again, but the violence of the fandango is here calmed to a gentle flattery." Sebastian Cerezo, a bailarin of the court of Charles III, who, coming from the throne of Naples, encouraged a certain Italianization in Spanish art, crystallized the steps of the Bolero into a set form, incorporating into it the style and technique then existing in the classical ballet, as well as the lively bouncing steps of its earlier form.

Anton Bolinche of Sevilla "fitted to the tempo and form of the Bolero whatever struck him as charming or outstanding in the Fandango and other dances of his time. This Bolero which he found only in the schools, he finished by leaving not only in the streets but also in the salons of the court." [9] And this dance which was first done only by the nobility very shortly found its way into the theater. The theater Bolero of Cerezo has enjoyed a popularity so long that it endures to this day and appears in the repertoire of most of the great Spanish dancers of this century. It might be well to note here how often the dances of Spain were ante-dated by the music which accompanied them. Typical of this is the tune of the Bolero which has been sung in Asturia from time immemorial. Or the Seguidillas which

[8] Havelock Ellis, "The Soul of Spain," Houghton Mifflin Co., 1909, London.
[9] José Otero, "Tratado de Bailes," Guia Oficial, 1912, Sevilla.

BOLERO—JOSÉ GRECO

BOLERO—THALIA MARA and ARTHUR MAHONEY

was a poetic form in the remote past and was sung as early as 1658,
and yet seems not to have been danced until about a century later.

Together with these divertissements appeared the Danzas Habladas
which were pantomimes on the style of the Masques of Ben Jonson.

The Cachucha, which had absorbed the Zarabanda and the Chacona
was, in turn, absorbed by the Seguidillas Manchegas, a popular dance
of La Mancha. Like the Fandango, it was danced by two couples and
was divided into coplas, each one of which finished in a proud immobile pose which wrung from the enthusiastic spectators a heartfelt
"bien parado" (well-posed). Lightness and accuracy of footwork
were much prized in this dance, and double and triple pirouettes were
not infrequent. This Seguidillas soon turned into a finer, more gracious
pastime by the aristocracy of Spain, whose appetite for newer and
gayer dances seemed insatiable. Coplas of the Seguidillas swept the
Peninsula. In Andalucia the dance became so popular that it was re-
formed and adopted as the typical dance of that region, the Sevillanas.

But the dance in the classic theater began to suffer under an excess
of form. Many books were written which set forth the rules of conduct and execution of Iberian choreography. From Pablo Minguet
(1716) to Carlo Blasis (1830), maestros were busy setting terminology and etiquette for the art. The spontaneous Spanish dance,
half gypsy that it is, could not thrive in this corset of form. Under
the baton of the ballet it rapidly broke down, leaving only the shell
of itself on the opera stage.

In the popular lyric theater the Zarzuela was succeeded by the
Zarzuelita (a one-act Zarzuela) and the Tonadilla. The "Tonadilla"
was a little song with guitar accompaniment, appended to one of the
minor theatrical forms. In the person of the "tonadillera," the dance
survived in the Spanish theater, for in 1776, Maria Fernandez of
Granada, "La Caramba," introduced a little dance into her Tonadilla;
thereafter, for a century-and-a-half the Spanish dancer was called a
"tonadillera" and it was expected of her to also sing.

"The Gitana" which Taglioni[10] danced in 1830 had little of the fire
of the original Fandango. But in 1834 Dolores Serral of the Royal
Theater of Madrid taught the Cachucha to an Austrian named Fanny
Elssler.[11] This sultry dancer, overleaping the barriers of form to grasp
the essential excitement of the Iberian art, surprised and inflamed all
Europe with her interpretation of the Cachucha and Fandango. The
enthusiastic Gautier[12] wrote of her with rhapsodic pen: "Now she
darts forward; the castanets begin their sonorous clatter; with her

[10] Maria Taglioni, 1804-1884.
[11] Fanny Elssler, 1810-1884.
[12] Théophile Gautier, 1811-1872.

hands she seems to shake down clusters of rhythm. How she twists! How she bends! What fire! What voluptuousness of motion! What eager zest! Her arms seem to swoon, her head droops, her body curves backward until her white shoulders almost graze the ground. What charm of gesture! And with that hand that sweeps over the dazzle of the footlights, would not one say that she gathered all the enthusiasms and all the desires of those who watch her?"

If half this dithyramb be true, it is small wonder that in New York our grandfathers unhitched her horses and themselves drew her carriage through the streets. For fifteen years she traveled the world introducing, for the first time, the popular Spanish dance. Her admirers were many, and so great was the rivalry between her and Taglioni that all London was divided into two cliques—the Elssler-rites and Taglionites. She herself felt this rivalry very keenly, and finally announced that she would appear in "La Sylphide," the ballet which was the "tour de force" of Taglioni. The "pas" of the classical ballet were unsuited to the temperamental Austrian, and after her appearance as the sylph, her popularity waned in London. On the continent very shortly afterwards her temperament again betrayed her. For several seasons after her return from America she danced at the Scala in Milan. One evening it was arranged that all the dancers of the ballet should wear medals which had recently been struck celebrating the Pope's blessing on a united Italy. Elssler, being Austrian, fancied this an insult to her nationality, and so she refused to go on the stage while the corps wore the offending medals. As soon as possible the dancers were instructed to remove the medals and the ballet was continued. But somehow the news reached the audience, and when Elssler finally appeared she was received with hisses. This was the beginning of the end of her fortune and soon the stages saw her no more.

As late as 1928 the great José Otero was still bitterly lamenting the passing of the style of dance-technique embodied in the Seguidillas and Sevillanas Boleras—the *cuartas*, the *lazos*, the elevation and the turns. In his "Tratado de Bailes" he wrote, "If, before 1870 one had said to a girl of Triana or San Bernardo or La Macarena 'Let us dance a waltz,' she would have said 'What nonsense!' . . . and it was not only in these quarters that it was considered almost an insult to dance, por lo fino, as they called it . . . but today there is not a one who does not know how to slide her feet along the floor, having lost those classic fiestas which it was a joy to behold."

Early in the twentieth century the "baile flamenco" appeared in the music halls of Spain. And the reason for its debut was this. Up to that time the professional dancers had depended largely on the

1. Campanelas 2. Embotadas 3. Paseo 4. Un pasar 5. Pistolces 6. Atabalillos, de las seguidillas boleras.

Estampas grabadas por Marcos Téllez

Courtesy A. Martin, Barcelona

SEGUIDILLAS—a series of prints

The popularity of the Seguidillas is shown in these charming eighteenth-century engravings. The dancers may belong to the aristocracy but in spite of their formal costumes and headdresses they dance the different coplas of the Seguidillas with enthusiasm and abandon.

JOSÉ OTERO

Bolero, the Fandango, etc., for repertoire. But one day a Negro from the United States appeared in a Barcelona "cafetin" dancing the Cakewalk. Inexplicably his success was immediate and overpowering. The popular native dances lost caste. The Spanish public desired nothing but the Cakewalk. According to Otero, it was a professional Spanish dancer displaced by the high-stepping colored boy, who went to the "cuevas" (caves) of the "gitanos" (gypsies) for new repertoire. Until then little had been seen of the Flamenco dance outside the "barrios" (gypsy quarters), save when the gypsy himself performed at street fairs to gather coppers. But the gypsy dancing for alien eyes was not the gypsy dancing for himself and his own. The Spanish professional determined to catch something of the elusive quality of controlled emotionalism which motivated the Flamenco dance, rightly guessing that it would speak directly to the heart of the passionate Iberian. I need not add that from the moment of its appearance, the "Baile Flamenco" was successful.

At about this time Otero was called to Stockholm to stage the ballet in "Carmen," and here the Spanish master became enthusiastic over the practical method of study offered by the ballet and the convenience of an accepted terminology. He incorporated the idea of regularized technical study into his school, and labored all his life to clarify the application of names which his countrymen had given various dance-steps. But few Spanish teachers today have adopted his method, preferring the old one of teaching through routines rather than through technique. Needless to say this is a difficult if not impossible method for the foreigner. With his system of clarified technique, Otero paved the way for the later classicization of the pure Spanish dance.

After the appearance of the Baile Flamenco in the cafetin, old favorites of the folk dances began to introduce "taconeo" (heelbeats), and other gypsy characteristics into their routines. This type of dance is called "agitanado" (gypsy-ized) and today there are few popular dances which are not agitanado.

While the tonadillera "La Tortajada" was captivating Berlin, Pepe Amayo and his troupe introduced the Flamenco dance to Paris at the Exposicion Universal (1900). Shortly thereafter, Amalia Molina, "reina de las castañuelas," traveled abroad, as did the majestic "La Goya" (both circa 1915), and the adored Pastora Imperio (circa 1920). Before 1920 Buenos Aires music halls cheered the singing-dancing-whistling tonadillera, La Argentina.

Popularly successful from her first appearance, Argentina toured Latin-America for many years. She came twice to the United States, but without success. She danced seven years unnoticed in the cafés of Paris, and all this time there were few (and these few artists) who recognized in her the outstanding creative genius of the Spanish dance. With a tenacity so courageous that it seems the grip of destiny, she never lost faith in her artistic ideal and never lost touch with her artistic integrity.

Just before the first World War there came into prominence several Spanish composers who used as themes for their compositions the popular melodies of the folk. Granados, Albeniz, De Falla and Turina, understanding and loving the music of their country, classicized it and made of it an undying art. Shortly after the close of the war, La Argentina, knowing every step and gesture and tradition of the Spanish dance, added to them her own rare genius, and inspired by the music of her illustrious fellow-countrymen, created the neo-classic Spanish dance.

Chapter

III

SCHOOL DANCE

A history never answers questions that are uppermost in a dancer's mind—not "when," so much as "how." To the average reader the dithyrambic prose of the contemporary writer is best for eventual visualization of a dance never seen or half-forgotten or misunderstood. But the dancer visualizes best through the cold facts of choreography and floor and air-designs. This chapter, then, is for the dancer.

The "school dance" is the dance taught in the dancing schools, from the courtly Pavane to the last composition of Otero in Sevilla.

The *Pavane*, one of the first of the "basses dances" (low dances—feet gliding on the floor) had its origin in Spain. "The ceremonious dignity, splendor and grave pride inherent in the steps and music of the Pavane are suggested by its name, which is derived from the Latin— pavo (peacock)." [1] "The Pavane sustained its popularity from about 1530 to 1676." . . . At the Spanish court it "was developed into a processional pageant of great dignity and imposing spectacle." [2] "The queens and princesses and great ladies accompany them (the king and princes and lords) with the long trains of their dresses let down and trailing behind them." [3]

"That the Pavane never became much more than a simple walking, with slight variations, is self-evident; the chief dictum required that

[1] Louis Horst, "Pre-Classic Dance Forms," The Dance Observer, 1940, New York.
[2] *Ibid.*
[3] "Dictionnaire de Trevour"—1721.

Photo by Diaz and Rogers

GOYESCA—ANTONIO and ROSARIO

'the students of this dance must enshroud their very souls with majestic dignity.' It was danced by one couple or many couples. Before beginning the dance the performers walked very gravely around the room and saluted the king and queen." [4]

Some authorities say that the gentleman holds the very tip of the lady's right hand in his left; others, that the couple did not touch hands, the gentleman keeping his right hand on his dagger-hilt and his left hanging "as though dead." Both Curt Sachs and Louis Horst give the full choreography of the pavane in their recent books, "World History of the Dance," and "Pre-Classic Dance Forms," respectively.

Important to our present chapter is the fact that with the pavane a vocabulary of steps appeared for the first time in dance history. With this vocabulary there sprung up all over cultured Europe dancing masters and schools for the correct teaching of these steps. At this period "courtly dance and folk dance are separated once for all. They will continue to influence each other but they have fundamentally different aims and different styles." [5]

The "untamed" gypsy Zarabanda, under the influence of the trained, set dances of the court, became very shortly the *Sarabande*. Like the pavane, the sarabande is danced with "gravity, pride, solemnity and religious and processional austerity." In spite of this essential solemnity, it was often danced with castanets. Couples walk four steps forward and four backward, and, changing places, form lines between which other couples walk. It is all very grave, but hands are lightly held, and even arms taken!

Toward the turn of the century the dance began to skip and kick lightly, to "turn away from the formality and flatness of civilization to the ebullience of the provincial." [6] So the style of this period includes a certain technical lightness of the lower limbs, and the arms, while still not lifting above shoulder-height, have more ease and movement. Some authorities believe the origin of the *Chacona* to be West Indian. It seems more likely that it went to America and there acquired certain attributes which then appeared also in Spain. For surely Spain had no need to go abroad to acquire that something "sensual and wild" which is said to have been a part of the early Chacona. In the seventeenth century it was considered the "most passionate and unbridled of all dances." But to understand what is meant by "unbridled" we must depart from the austerity of the sarabande

[4] Horst, *op. cit.*
[5] Curt Sachs, "World History of the Dance," W. W. Norton & Co., Inc., 1937, New York.
[6] *Ibid.*

and from the background, conscious and sub-conscious, of our own times.

The *"pas de chaconne"* is a step forward on the left foot with a light swing of the right leg forward and across; a quarter turn right and a cabriole left finishing in a fifth position with the right foot in front, then the right leg swings high as the body completes the turn. This is indeed an "alta danza" (high dance—jumped). Horst tells us that "when the court grew tired of it, it found a place on the stage." An early description of the Chacona as a theater-dance gives the following choreography: a gypsy girl enters with castanets and dances; then a magician enters and with his wand transfixes her into immobility while he dances, finally he releases her from the spell and they both dance together. Could this be the earliest example of the dance-form of three coplas and of the immobility of the *bien parado* which concluded each?

Most authorities believe that the Spanish *Pasacalle* is simply a Chacona of more deliberate and less emotional movement. Certainly Despereaux's poetic description of Louis XIV dancing a Pasacalle has little to do with kicks and cabrioles.

> *In the costume of a God, dancing solo at Versailles*
> *With grave, majestic steps, the solemn Passacaille.*

Circa 1690 the *Folia* (madness) was mentioned as a theater dance but said to be without "pas réglés." Folia was originally a Portuguese fertility dance and as far as can be ascertained was rather in the style of a regional Jota. Transformed into a courtship dance and performed with castanets, it seems to have enjoyed a wide if short popularity. Certainly after its appearance Spain turned away from the stately "pas" of the Pavane and Sarabande.

At this point it is well to recall that the Zarzuela came into being in 1657, since it surely greatly affected the style of dancing. The court dance, the street dance and the regional dance were to be looked at by spectators in a circle around and on a level with the dancers. The advent of choreography into the theater placed the watchers below and on one side, or in some cases on three sides of the dancers. Choreography surely changed to fit this new development. And with the democratic popularity of the Zarzuela, the dance obviously took on a gayer note.

The technical style which characterizes the Chacona remains relatively unchanged until the theatricalization of the Fandango and Bolero. According to written sources the *Fandango* appeared in Spain in 1750, but some say it originated as early as 1000. Performed by a

Año 1830. — Paso de *Fandango*

Grabado francés

Courtesy A. Martin, Barcelona

FANDANGO—an engraving

man and woman, it is a courtship dance which "rushes on deliri-
ously." [7] The two dancers never touch each other, but the whole
dance is an inflaming challenge in pantomime, which could have been
inspired only by a race imbibed with orientalism.

The arms are carried with the elbows at shoulder height, the hands
manipulate castanets or make "pito" (snap fingers). The feet are occupied with steps of *esplantes, jota, vuelta en cuatro tiempos, vuelta
de tornillo, cachuchas, gorgollatas.* Tapping heels in the Fandango
are noted by Iriarte in the late eighteenth century. Danced by two
couples in a square, the choreography is set in three coplas and features the passes which characterize the Sevillanas. Versions of the
dance exist in Spain today in Extremadura, Asturia, Old Castile and
the Basque country.

The solo of the miller's wife in De Falla's "Three-Cornered Hat"
is a Fandango; and one of Argentinita's loveliest dances was the Fandango in her "Sketches from Goya" produced at New York's Metropolitan Opera House, in the repertoire of Ballet Theater in 1943.
Argentinita herself told me that the melody from the second act of
"Carmen" was taken from an old Fandango.

In the nineteenth century the Fandango disappeared, being considered too exuberant and sensual. Its place was taken by the Bolero
which was formalized or, some say, invented by Cerezo in 1780.

The *Bolero* is a couple dance of courtship without the sensual challenge of the Fandango—a light, bright, elegant theater-piece. The
"brazeo" (arm-carriage) is much the same as that of the Fandango,
castanets or chinchines being used. But the lower limbs become in-
creasingly important with the refinement of the regional "batterié"
and the exciting air-work of the ballet—*cuartas, lazos, emboteados,
matalarañas, piruetas, cuatropeados, cabrioles,* etc. Because of this
technique, it is generally, though not always, danced in heelless slip-
pers. Very rarely it is danced on point.

It is set in three coplas. The first and third coplas are a duet; the
second can be danced either "liso" (solo) or "robado" (the two
dancers alternating in solos). It features the "paseo di gracia" (entrance walk) and the bien parado still seen in the Sevillanas.

Both Argentina and Argentinita included a classic Bolero in their
repertoire and the first movement of Argentinita's interpretation of
Ravel's "Bolero" is based on this classic dance. Of contemporary
dancers the finest protagonist of the Bolero is Pilar Lopez, whose
lightness and batterié is without equal. Among male dancers, Federico
Rey, who first appeared in this country with Argentinita gives to

[7] *Ibid.*

Photo by Antonio, Zaragoza

PILAR LOPEZ in "Bolero"

the Bolero an elevation and staccato brilliancy which makes him out-standing.

The Bolero has been used by Auber in "Mansanillo"; by Carl Maria von Weber in "Preciosa"; and by Mihul and Delibes. Ravel's "Bolero" is a descriptive piece which has nothing to do with the period dance.

Toward the middle of the century the *Seguidillas Manchegas* caught up the waning popularity of the Bolero. The Seguidillas is light and gay, the flirtation is more direct and bucolic than in the Bolero, and not so wild and sensual as in the Fandango. The brazeo is generally a wide "Y," or, sometimes, like that of the Bolero. The feet are light and play around each other, characteristic steps being: *manchegas, seguidillas, lazos, emboteados, matalarañas, piruetas, pasadas, malagueñas,* etc.

It is danced by one or two couples (a form which it doubtless takes from the Fandango) in coplas (generally three), and features the "paseo" (walk around) and bien parado.

Today a form of the Seguidillas still exists in Old Castile and in Galicia.

Argentinita's ensemble featured a Seguidillas among their school-dance suite, as does my own dance-group.

Bizet's "Near to the Walls of Sevilla" is an adaptation of the Seguidillas tempo.

For many years the Seguidillas remained a way of teaching neat footwork in the Spanish schools, "for Spanish maestros have usually imparted their teaching through actual dances. Such a procedure seems hopelessly crude to the modern idea, and for the ballet it would be ludicrous, but with this highly individual art it certainly succeeded, and it is equally certain that the pupils would never have submitted to large doses of preliminary technique." [8]

"The dance which has best survived this vanished Golden Age is that offshoot of the Seguidillas group known as the Sevillanas. . . ." [9]

Fifty years ago there was a Sevillanas Boleras which featured the batterié of the original Bolero, but within three decades it passed into oblivion and only the Seguidillas Sevillanas remained in the dancing academies of Andalucia. In 1900 the *Seguidillas Sevillanas,* not yet agitanado, was danced with rounded arms, bounced rather than stepped, and with a minimum of light "golpes" (foot stamp). The routine of this period is given in full in Otero's book "Tratado de Bailes," the music and floor design remaining the same as it is today. If agitanado, the floor design is tightened up and the body spirals on itself, especially in the *panaderos;* the arms are neither wide in the

---

[8] Cyril Rice, "Dancing in Spain," British Continental Press, 1931, London.
[9] *Ibid.*

Photo by Philcox

SEVILLANAS *circa* 1900—LILIAN

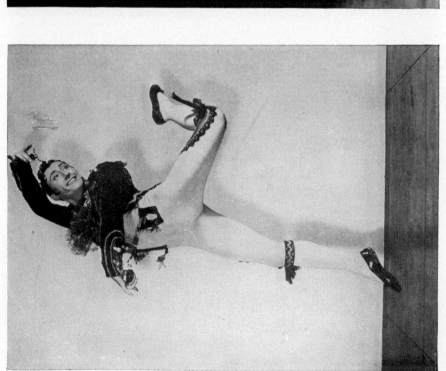

FEDERICO REY in "Bolero"

style introduced by Argentina, nor "a la morisco" (Moorish style) as the gypsies use them. The taconeo is sharp, and the whole style returns to the sensuality which inflamed the Fandango.

With the Sevillanas we must, per forza, close the list of dances which can be described in some detail. From Cerezo, the school dance has been created by the individual maestro. There are literally hundreds of school dances whose popularity lifted them briefly into the pages of history. Surely hundreds, failing to catch the public fancy, have been forgotten. In Andalucia the school dance and the regional dance overlapped in such a way that it is difficult to tell one from the other. Capmany names the Fandanguillo a "folk dance" of Andalucia, and yet Otero himself taught it to me as his own composition. The Marianas is often considered a regional dance of Andalucia, yet Otero writes that he first saw it danced in 1904 by Argentinita! That is how close we are to the amazing transformation of the dance of Spain from a popular pastime into an established art form.

Dozens of titles come to the memory of dances which were once taught in Sevilla and performed by every artist and amateur in that dance-mad city—the Soleares de Arcas, Las Guajiras, Gracia de Sevilla, Panaderos, Peteneras, Fandanguillos, Jaleo con Peteneras and Escenas Gitanas.

Famous tonadilleras of this period were La Goya and Amalia Molina (once partnered by Beaucaire-Montalvo), who first appeared in Madrid in 1902. Many of the routines were preserved in the school of Beaucaire-Montalvo, who was a pupil of Otero a half-century ago.

There are school dance versions of many of the spontaneous gypsy dances. Notable among these is the Garrotin which the gypsies themselves now seldom dance. But there exist various interpretations of the Farruca, the Tango, the Zapateado and Zambra. Many of these are now with castanets, which, fifty years ago, the gypsy did not use.

Those of us who studied with old Otero know the great school dances of his day: Fandanguillo, Asturiana Soy, Del Sacro-Monte, Tango de Cadiz, etc. These, together with the Sevillanas, were danced not only by all Otero's pupils at fiestas in street and square, but by the professional dancers in cafetin and theater.

Chapter

IV

R E G I O N A L   (North)

*T*he regions of Spain are filled with sounding names of folk dances whose origins are lost in pagan antiquity and the songs which accompany these dances are still sung hauntingly on street-corners in the little sun-parched villages. Pilgrims since 1600 B.C. until today have gone over Iberia, seeking the magic of her dances and have tried to capture them with sketches and photographs, with music and choreographic notation. There are many volumes written in Spanish which are painstakingly devoted to descriptions of these myriad Iberian folk dances. But the written material is dry and dead, just as the enthusiastic dithyrambs are tantalizingly unclear.

How shall I describe the colorful regional dances of Spain? This chapter has been rewritten many times and never to the satisfaction of the dancer. After twenty pages the names and the descriptions blur together, and one becomes convinced that there is little difference between the one and the other. Choreographically there are round dances, there are dances in lines and there are couple dances. Many of the round dances are of Greek origin; many of the line dances ante-date even Hellenic days; many of the couple dances originated in the Fandango, which is said to have been influenced if not inspired by the Phoenicians. Then again, who will tell me if the Spaniard dances today as he did before his revolution? Do the folk still gather on the plaza after church to dance the Chun-Chun, the Jota and the Sardana? A revolution and a great war have passed over Spain, and the movies, the radio and foreign commercialism have entered. Do the old folk teach the Giraldilla to the youngsters?

Photo by Bruno of Hollywood

COSTUMES OF ASTURIA
ARGENTINITA, FEDERICO REY and PILAR LOPEZ

Or is it already fading into history to join the Zarabanda and the Mauresque?

Ruth Anderson writes that often at fiestas the typical orchestras play two-steps and fox-trots; or, that to the music of the Muiñeira natives will take the floor, some dancing the Muiñeira while others dance a closed two-step. Of the modern Muiñeira itself "Our neighbor explained that this dance was the muiñeira which takes its name from the Gallegan word for mill (muiño). We said it was very pretty, but he sighed for the decorum the muiñeira used to have. It was originally a pantomime, almost religious, of courtship in which the girl, keeping her arms low and her eyes fixed on the ground, danced quietly and modestly while her partner wove about her all the extravagancies he could devise. This girl had laughed and flirted while she was dancing; he did not know what they were coming to! By a most unfortunate deterioration of taste the modern round dance (agarradino) with its vulgar immodest clinch was destroying the dignity and sobriety of the classic regional dances!" [1]

Aurelio Capmany writes, "To give the picture its true value it is necessary to imagine the Iberian Peninsula divided into three main regions or sections, which could be termed northern, central and southern. The differences between the dances of the first section and those of the third are so obvious that in no other country can one find an example of such diversity. From the Mediterranean to the Atlantic, following a line parallel to the Pyrenees and as far as the Cantabrian Sea, we find dances of a certain similarity or kinship, as though they had a common origin. Though the character is different the same can be said of the extensive region of Andalucia; and the intermediary region, besides having much of its own partakes to a certain extent of the characteristics of the other two.

"This difference between the two regions is so fundamental that it represents as comprehensive a classification as that of differing emotionalisms. A foreigner assisting at a display of regional dances of the north always allowing a few exceptions, would simply admire the tranquil, sober grace of the movements. In those of the south, the "bailador" (male dancer) and most especially the "bailarina" (female dancer), produces quite a different effect on the spectator; she is exciting, provocative and sensual, while his "variedades" (virtuosities) achieve an international popularity such as will probably never be attained by the northerners.

"The two types present yet another distinguished trait; the dances of the north are usually collective, while those of the south are for

[1] Ruth Anderson, "Pontevadra and La Coruña," Hispanic Society of America, 1939, New York.

the most part individual. . . . All this being true it would not be
hazardous to affirm that in Spain exists the greatest variety and mul-
tiplicity of that art of rhythmic movement called "baile" or "danza"
(dance) and consequently to Spain may be ascribed the maternity of
the dance." [2]

The folk dance holds a triple value to history since it is:—first, the
most sincere reflection of the psychology of a people at the time of
its invention; second, it reveals much of the habits and customs
of the people as well as their practical evolution; third, it is the dance
from which inevitably grows both in technique and spirit the dance-
art of a nation. These are the dances which are herein reviewed.

In a nation of such prodigious choreographic output as Spain it
would take several volumes to list each and every dance and do such
justice to it that it becomes for the reader a living thing. Ergo, it has
been necessary to ignore those dances which are little more than
marching or capering at the head of religious processions. Although
these spectacles have great interest for the ethnologist, showing as
they often do, the superimposition of Catholicism on mysterious ancient pagan rites, yet they have given little or nothing to the evolution of the dance-art and so, in this little book, may be overlooked.

ASTURIA claims to have the oldest dance of Spain and calls it La
Danza Prima. This is a simple round dance with men and women
alternating in the circle, and is, according to Inzenga y Castellanos,
like the Hebraic choral dances of biblical times. "Some say the Danza
Prima is a round dance of the Greeks described by Homer; others
say that it proceeds from the "Chorea" of which San Isidore speaks in
his "Etymologies"; some compare it to the pyrrhic dances, and finally
there are those who, remembering that most ancient dances were
symbolic or even dramatic for the people who perfomed them, see
in the one under discussion a parody of the ceremony used at the
"juramento" (oath-taking) of the Gothic kings." [3] The verses of the
ballad which accompany the dance are each preceded by an interjec-
tion which dedicates that movement to the Virgin, or to a saint, and
during the dance the executants, becoming excited, utter from time
to time the druidical call of "hi-ju-ju."

The Danza Prima was created for the happiness of the performer—
not the admiration of the spectator. And yet, since all dances are
malleable to the folk, it can be done with a vigorous enthusiasm that
notably enhances it. Originally performed before going into battle,

[2] Aurelio Capmany, "Folklore y Costumbres de España," Vol. II (El Baile y
La Danza), Casa Editorial, Alberto Martin, 1934, Barcelona.
[3] Ibid.

Photo by Elite Studio

VAQUERO of AUSTRIA—JUAN BEAUCAIRE-MONTALVO

Capmany says that at one time the execution of the Danza Prima so
excited the dancers that it often ended in fights. Finally, so as to put
an end to the riots, there was a law passed prohibiting its performance.

The Danza Prima is called Danza de San Pedro when it is executed
on that saint's feast day; or, Danza de San Pablo, de San Roque, de la
Magdalena, when celebrated on such feast days. In Candas it is danced
exclusively by women.

The *Xirenguelo* is another popular dance of Asturia of far more
recent date, since it is an import (the Fandango) from Castile. Like
the Fandango it is danced with more gaiety than grace by four or
five couples who start simply enough, but as copla succeeds copla the
dancing becomes more and more complicated. The choreography
is like that of the Baile de Pandero (said to have originated with
the "vaqueros") which begins with a "patagueya" (salute) in which
the man approaches his partner and executes a turn, which is the
classic beginning of the Fandango, the Seguidillas and the Sevillanas.
The floor design is built on a line of men and of women, each facing
his partner, and all with castanets for accompaniment. The dance
takes its name from the pandero which is beaten to accent and ac-
celerate the rhythm. The old people execute the Pandero in a more
sedate style and call it Fandango Punteado.

The vaqueros of Asturia perform nameless but athletic male solos
to the accompaniment of castanets and pandero (or, failing the latter,
with a large key struck against a skillet). These vaqueros are, so to
speak, cowboys and are of a race apart—some say Moorish, some say
Roman. Certainly their dances are exotic to the general Spanish
choreography.

The *Careado* consists of two parts; a. "entrada" (entrance) and
patagueya, b. the Giraldilla. In the first movement partners face
each other in two long lines and sing all together while moving the
body rhythmically from side to side. The *Giraldilla* (which is sometimes executed apart from the Careado) is more definitely a couple
dance with castanets akin to the Fandango but far simpler, although
it employs the difficult *lazos*. When the oldsters do the Giraldilla
they rename it the *Perlindango*. The name Perlindango derives from
the apron worn by the women on Sunday and holidays, and which
they wave while dancing certain steps.

The *Salton* is a fast and violent variation of the Fandango.

The *Baile de los Pollos* is a social variation of the Giraldilla. Two
boys enter the circle and invite two girls to dance with them. They
dance in a square for the duration of the song. Then the boys retire
and the girls left in the circle choose new partners. Thus alternating

Courtesy the Hispanic Society of America

"The Galician Dance" by Alvarez de Sotomayor, 1875

It is summer. Young and old join in the festivity of the dance. The picture portrays the character of the Galician people, the somber expression on some faces and the attentive pleasure on others as they follow the movements of the Muiñeira Gallega.

they arrive at the point where there are no more partners to choose, and the last two "quedan pollos" (remain chickens).

The *Corri-Corri* is typical of the village of Arenas. It is danced by a man and six women who carry laurel branches with which they alternately ward off the man and beckon him to them. Capmany says this dance merits the attention of ethnologists, and certainly there is a pagan ritualistic atmosphere suggested by the choreography.

The *Pericote* is danced by a man and two women (*vide* the Zangano of Valencia) and is a lively and colorful dance which abounds in a variety of figures. Sometimes—as when so many young men emigrated to Mexico—a young woman, wearing a man's hat decorated in ribbons, takes the man's part.

To the list of pantomimically flirtatious dances should be added; the Baila de la Reposa (a circular dance), the Rebudixu (couples), the Jota of Oviedo and the Generingosa, the Asturian version of the A Lo Llano of Burgos.

GALICIA. Inzenga y Castellanos claim that the *Muiñeira Gallega* resembles the pyrrhic dances described by Homer, while Martinez Padin says it is a survival of Greek custom. Still other authorities believe it to be an ancient war-song of the Suevos, or of the Brigantinos who worshiped the moon, or ascribe to it a remote Celtic origin. Certainly it reflects in allegory "the whole history of Love," [4] the feminine modesty and masculine gallantry of courtship, and the fidelity and felicity of married life. In the first movement the man begins to dance with great agility and acrobacy, trying, as it were, to impress his chosen partner. Before her, he eventually prostrates himself on one knee. Then the two dance together, she modestly and with eyes cast down, he still leaping and turning. This is the courtship. Other couples join in the dance until all are moving. Then the women form a circle, while the men form another outside it, and these two circles move in opposite directions to the accompaniment of castanets.

Sometimes the dancers form lines instead of circles. Sometimes two male dancers step out and contest each other for choreographic supremacy. (This is the communal life of marriage.) At the end, the couples again find each other, dance briefly and gently together, and the dance is over. The second figure of the Muiñeira is called the "contrapaso" and is often danced without the preceding and succeeding duet movements.

The character of the Muiñeira is a strong admixture of melancholy

[4] Inzenga y Castellanos, "Bailes y Cantos Populares de España," A. Romero A., 1888, Madrid.

and delight which well suits the Gallego who is of a marked Celtic type, both in feature and mentality. The Gallego is filled with poetry and superstition and, being introspective, is declared by the rest of Spain to be terribly stupid.

All through Galicia pantomime and round dances abound which exalt spring, love, and the beauties of nature. These may be danced by little girls or boys. Or young people may dance with swords, arches and be-ribboned poles, the celebration of the coming of spring.

Otero spoke of a dance called the Gallegada, and described it as a gay rather gauche dance in which boy and girl bump posteriors in the manner of the Zandango of Castile. Juan Martinez describes the Gallegada as danced: the woman, serious—the man, comic. Cyril Rice says the Gallegada is "the same type as the Muiñeira, and also in 6/8 time" and that it is "apparently rapidly disappearing." [5] Other authorities claim the Gallegada to be only the name of the music which accompanies the Muiñeira, although we know from Ribera's statement that the Muiñeira is of classical antiquity in northern Spain. Capmany gives the Gallega as the most popular dance of Galicia, saying that it is also called Magosto or Baila, and that it is "serious and elegant." He says the Muiñeira is like the Giraldilla of Asturia and is also called the Contrapas.

There is also the *Boleras de los Gallegos* which begins as a circle with all holding hands; then all turn to make couples, the man facing the girl on his right; here they execute a sort of Jota, and making a half-turn, change partners; comes the "cadena" (chain), the "puente" (bridge) and the circle is broken to dance the Jota in couples.

SANTANDER is compared to the rest of Spain, amazingly poor choreographically. Her dance is *Las Pasiegas* which begins with great dignity with the men in a row facing the women. They take a few steps forward, a few backward and then swing their partners. As the dance proceeds the men warm up and begin to kick and bound and turn, while the women remain modestly grave and take only an occasional glimpse of their partners through downcast lashes. Variations of Las Pasiegas are danced in Guipuzco, Zamora, Aragon, Valencia and Murcia.

The mountain dances of Santander seem to be more of a grave ceremonial act, than a pleasure or diversion. The dance is divided in two parts and begins with a slow *zarandeo* or swaying of the body from side to side, with an air of incantation. At a sudden signal from the music, the dancers spring into action, faces light-up, eyes meet and couples burst into a lively duet in which the men execute all types

[5] Cyril Rice, "Dancing in Spain," British Continental Press, 1931, London.

of intricate foot-work while the women follow them with amazing precision. (*Vide* the Careado of Asturia.)

THE BASQUE PROVINCES. The Basques are stubbornly insular, and claim to be neither Spanish nor French ... but Basque! According to findings of Professor Marr, the Basques are of a race which can trace its purity back 8000 years, since their language identifies them with the Japhetic peoples, which included the Phrygians, the Philistines, the Etruscans and the Pelasgians. Rodney Gallop writes of the Basques; here "one may study all that is left of an older Europe, vanished elsewhere but lingering yet awhile in this quiet corner of the Pyrenees." Strabo, the Greek geographer and historian, has also written of the Basque dance.

The most popular recreational dance among the Basques is the *Aurresku,* which according to Gallop, is not only spectacular, but somewhat erotic. The title is derived from the aurresku, or leader, who begins the dance by sending four men to fetch his chosen partner. Before this partner the aurresku dances the "entra," or "tonda," in which he shows off all his best feats. The second movement is called "atzescu" (meaning "tail") and is danced in one long line with the dancers holding hands or the opposite corners of a handkerchief. At the head of the line is the aurresku, and at the end the atzescu, and each one shows his skill in complicated steps. The third movement is the "Zortzico," which is taken from the sword dance. The dancers form a circle, holding hands with squared-off brazeo, and move in a simple step, while the aurresku, in the center, executes all those amazing feats of choreographic agility which have been adopted by our modern ballet: tour en l'air, pirouettes, cabrioles, brises, entrechats, etc. All this display of technique is offered with expressionless face and rigid upper-body.

The fourth movement of the Aurresku is the "pasamano," (grand right and left). Then comes the "desafio" (challenge). Here the line divides into two sections which advance toward each other. Aurresku and atzescu are opposite and as they approach they leap as high as they can (which in itself may be of ritualistic origin; as high as a man leaps, so high grow his crops). Here is interjected (since 1770) the Arin-arin, or Fandango, both of which are variations of the Jota Aragonesa.

The *Sauts Basques* is also danced by men and women and is now recreational, although its origin is ritualistic. According to De Lancre, the "witch-hunter," the Sauts was a sort of licentious Branle danced at the witches sabbath. The Sauts is better known in the French

Photo by Earle Forbes

BASQUE DANCE—FEDERICO REY

provinces of the Basque country than in the Spanish. Indeed, the variation of this dance best known in Spain is the Multidanzak of Navarra.

There are many spectacular and ritualistic dances in the Basque provinces, all of them executed exclusively by men. The *Sword Dances* of Guipuzco and Vizcaya are performed by young men trained from childhood in the difficult technique. With a leader who does all manner of astonishing air-work, the dancers spring lightly about with first one and then another of various dance-properties such as small and large hoops, sticks, etc. Similar to the Sword Dances is the Hoe-Dance; and tribes of gypsies wander about the country-side dancing a version of the ancient Mauresque.

Space prevents the listing of the many carnival dances made beautiful by colorful costumes, and by the pirouettes and air-work which invariably embellish the Basque dancing.

NAVARRA. Navarra lies like a link between the Basque provinces and Aragon, partaking a little of the qualities of each, and blending together the diversities of their characters and arts. "The Navarros are everywhere noted for their high ideals and for their patriotism. The men are of strong honesty and of valor without limit; hard workers but at the same time almost childlike in their enthusiasm for all that is of sane and healthy athletic amusement. The women are conceded to be the most intelligent of Spain; of strong and fine physique they are given much to attain culture whenever they are able. These assets of character in the Navarros have much to do with the charm, vigor and grace of El Chun-Chun which is their most characteristic dance.[6] The Chun-Chun is a variation of the Jota Aragonesa, differing little from it save that it is slower in tempo and somewhat heavier in movement. This is the dance with which Manuel De Falla closes his ballet of the "Sombrero de Tres Picos."

The *Multidanzak* is the name which the Navarros give to the Sauts Basques, which, according to Gallop are "neither wholly ritualistic nor purely recreational. Though they are danced on any Sunday or feast day and at weddings and similar occasions, men alone take part in them and there is something about the stiffness and gravity of the dancers which suggests archaic ceremonial rites. With light springing steps in no way acrobatic, yet difficult by reason of their intricacy, the whole circle moves round a few paces to the right then turns about and moves to the left again."

[6] Isobel de Palencia, "El Traje Regional de España," B. T. Batsford, Ltd., 1926, London.

"Aragon" by Sorolla y Bastida, 1863-1923

ARAGON, with her bouncing *Jota Aragonesa*, has won a place in the western dance world second only to Andalucia. Yet some writers claim that the Jota is of Basque origin, taking its name from "jotu" (Basque for "play upon an instrument"). Another author claims that the Jota was an old dance of the Canary Islands called "Canario," while others think the name comes from "sotar" (to jump) or that it was invented by a 12th century poet and musician named Aben Jot. Whatever the origin may be, the Jota Aragonesa is now a perfect vehicle of expression for the Aragonese character which is proud, independent, stubborn, forceful and intensely energetic.

Cyril Rice writes, "the one exception to the statement that Spanish dancing is Andalucian dancing writ large is the Jota of Aragon.... It has no pretention to grace, is hardy, athletic and humorous." The coplas which accompany the Jota are also "hardy and humorous": — "Your arms are lovely, like sausages they look, hung from the kitchen ceiling by the cook." Or again, "Everytime I see your garters, my eyes shine like candles."

Jotas of upper and central Aragon are "mas jota," "mas saltadora" (more leaped) than those of bajo Aragona, which are simple and keep the feet discreetly on the ground.

The men carry their arms squared off with the elbows as high as the shoulder. The women generally carry theirs a little lower. Performed on village square or threshing floor, the music is played almost incessantly and the dancers spring up to dance as long as their energy permits, ceasing only when another livelier couple or soloist begins. It is said that the Jota, "the fastest dance in the world," is less a dance than an endurance contest. Certainly ability is more admired than grace. Garcia Arista [7] writes that there can be no jota without song, and that the song was introduced to rest the dancers; though, nowadays they dance also during the song. Cyril Rice attributes to "a jovial priest" the belief that Aragonesas are "fallen angels, who, with their broken wings attempted to regain Heaven through the Jota."

Ellis in "The Soul of Spain," claims the Jota Aragonesa to be the "most important and lyrical dance outside Andalucia."

Certainly of all the dances of northern Spain it is the one which has been most used by the theater dancer. Escudero, the flamenco, danced it with his partner and it was one of Argentinita's most beloved and lovely numbers. There are a variety of typical steps which can be routined at the will of the dancer. Pilar Lopez tells me the finest performers make variations and combinations of the classic steps. I have

[7] Garcia Arista—monograf "La Jota"—Aurelio Capmany, "El Baile y La Danza" (Volume II, Folklore y Costumbres de España), Casa Editorial, Alberto Martin, 1934, Barcelona.

Photo by Walter E. Owen

DANCES OF ARAGON—PILAR GOMEZ

DANCES OF ARAGON—FEDERICO REY

seen it danced by an Aragonese couple "closed" and with liveliness and discretion to a fast Viennese waltz in the international ballroom of a transatlantic liner.

CATALUNYA, which the Catalunians say is in Spain but not of it, has also felt strongly the imprint of the Greek culture which flourished on its shores. Tenacious and proud, the Catalunians have clung for centuries to their purity of race, neither accepting the Spaniard, nor tolerating the French in this epoch; and no doubt, refusing Phoenician, Greek and Carthaginian in the past. Their Sardana is, in the words of Enric Morera, more than a dance: it is "a hymn, a song; it is Catalunya."

It seems strange to us to whom the communal dance is only a gracious pastime, that it could mean so much. But we must remember that to the "paysano" (peasant) his dance is an outpouring of his feelings, and he has no other channel than this. Whatever religion, love, patriotism, or beauty he feels, he, inarticulate part of the inarticulate soil, expresses at last in his dance—not only in Catalunya, but in all Spain. In all the world, the national dance is a hymn to God and country.

First written mention of the *Sardana* is found late in the 16th century, but everyone knows that it is of Greek origin. In the 17th century it found its way briefly into the courts. The contemporary choreography of the Sardana was set by a tailor-musician called "Pep" Ventura. The steps are simple enough, composed of longs and shorts to the right and left; the main difficulty is the mathematical one of keeping in mind the multiples of each step. But the circle of the Sardana, whether large or small, rings with a feeling so ritualistic that Primo de Rivera, trying to stamp out separatism, issued an order (1923) that it should not be danced unless a flag of Spain flew in the center of the group. There are two forms of the Sardana (besides the short and long), Ampurdanes and Selvata, named from the districts in which they originated. There seems to be little difference except that one starts to the right (Selvata) and the other to the left (Ampurdanes). Yet in Gerona, which is the center of the Sardanistas of both districts, the arguments as to which form is correct have become so warm that local authorities have had to intervene in the interests of public peace.

The *Contrapas* is the twin brother of the Sardana. It is probable that it was originally religious (of the "monjes" (monks) of Ariente), and like the Sardana is danced in a hand-holding circle. But the Contrapas is enlivened by steps called "trencato" (broken, or quick shuffling of the feet), "camades" (leg swings) and "girats" (turns).

Photo by Valente

COSTUMES OF CATALUNYA—
ARGENTINITA, PILAR LOPEZ, FEDERICO REY

Both Sardana and Contrapas are danced to couplets which describe the Passion of Jesus. Capmany has filled ten pages with exhaustive information on each and every dance of this region. From this let us glean the outstanding information on Catalunian choreography.

There are a good number of *Balls* listed, all of which seem to have stemmed from the Ball de Palau. The Ball Pla (or ballet) which is a couple dance; the Ballet de Deu which is performed by two lines of men dancers who move very simply forward and backward; and the Bal Cerda which is a composite of the two aforementioned. The Bal Cerda is known in northern Catalunya as the Ball dels Aranyous and in Barcelona as the Ball Rodo.

Of couple dances there are: the *Corranda* from the north of Catalunya which is acrobatic in style, involving the "camada rodoña" in which the man kicks over his partner's head, lifts her upward to arm's length while she kisses another girl similarly held high and other adagio lifts and poses; the Jota al Aire of Tarragona, less acrobatic but similar; La Castaña, the clapping dance of Lerida; the Morisco of the 15th century; and the Eixida (La Salida).

The *Bolangera* is a "wheel" dance, and derives its name from the word "bo" which means good. It had popularity in Catalunya and although of folk origin, in 1856 figured among the court dances. It is claimed that it dates from the 14th century, and that no lesser individual than the Abbot of the Monastery of Montserrat opened the dance in those times.

The *Mocador* is a handkerchief dance in which four girls give handkerchiefs to four boys to choose them as partners; after dancing, the girls retire and the four boys then give the handkerchiefs to four other girls; and so on until all have danced. The form recalls the Baile de los Pollos of Asturia, but the significance of the handkerchief as a means of choosing a partner might have its origin in the North African dancer's presentation of a handkerchief to a chosen lover.

A number of street dances have interesting and somewhat remote origins. *La Gala* of Campdevonal is said to have originated in certain symbolical representations of feudal customs of the Middle Ages. In it a single young man, wearing a typical costume and hat, dances with whatever woman comes into the square and desires to dance. As he finishes dancing with each, he sprinkles her with perfumed water. The Baile de las Nyacras, or dance of the oyster-shells, is surely of Greek origin. The Ball de Llet (pail of milk), in which the dancers try to kick over the pail of milk in the center of the circle, is doubtless an ancient fertility dance; as is Les Marratxes, or breaking of pitchers; and Porro, danced with earthenware jugs of wine balanced on the head; or the Ball de la Teya in which a live tree burned in the

center of a great fire recalls the sacrificial fires of pagan days; and
L'hereu Riera, a man's solo danced over crossed sticks—surely once
crossed swords.

There are other popular names: the square dance of Indiot (pea-
cock); the Farandole of Montserrat; the Aubada from the valley of
Aran; the Danses, choreographed for three, a man and two girls; the
Gala Gambeto, and many others which differ very little from the
Sardana and the Jota.

Chapter

V

R E G I O N A L   (Central)

*C*ASTILE. The dance claimed most popular in New Castile is the *Bolero*. Indeed so widespread was the acclaim accorded it that it was at one time called the national dance of Spain. Its exact origin is uncertain, but it would seem most possible that it evolved, like the Fandango and the Cachucha, from a combination of the Chacona and the Zarabanda. Its aspect as a school dance has been treated in chapter III. Suffice it to say, in the Capitol it became so much a dance of the folk that it spread all over the peninsula.

Scarcely less popular than the Bolero in Castile is the *Fandango*. Some authorities claim it owes its origin to the American Indians, and that it arrived in Europe as late as the seventeenth century. Others believe it to date back as far as the Phoenicians. Perhaps all these elements went into its making, together with the inimitable Spanish flare for choreography. Adopted by folk far from Castile they change the name of the Fandango to Malagueña, Murciana, Granadina or Rondeña.

The Fandango resembles in character and construction the Seguidillas Manchegas. First called Seguidillas Boleras, it appeared in La Mancha early in the 18th century. The lower limbs were quick and active under a body "asentao" (serene) and with widespread arms. Capmany is of the opinion that the dance itself was not invented in La Mancha, but only the step which characterizes it, yet all authorities agree that the Andalucian version does not change it save to make it more lively. If this be true, then, the choreographic pattern of dancing in coplas, each finishing with the bien parado and the character of the couple's advance and retreat is the same as the now widely-known Seguidillas Sevillanas, and follows the pattern of the old Fandango.

"It is certain that, be it Manchegas, Sevillanas, Chambregas or Boleras, the Seguidillas is purely and popularly Spanish . . . with a few variations, giving more liveliness to the turns, more freedom to the movements, more grace to the motion of the thighs, and more ease to the bending of the legs and the arching of the arms, the Seguidillas has been, and still is, the most genuinely Spanish of Spanish dances. On this account it has been the one which has best adapted itself to the traffic of the ages and the incessant evolution of custom without becoming disfigured or extinguished." [1] Soriano Fuertes declares the Seguidillas to be the oldest dance of Spain after the Danza Prima. "The great variety of its figures, a modest grace and much verve without license makes of this dance the most modest and at the same time the most gay of dances." [2]

La Charrada is the typical dance of the "charros" (Salamancans) and is the same as Leon's El Bailao. It is a couple dance executed with body and arms steady and with marked intricacies of the lower limbs, the man sometimes executing the "squat-fling" steps peculiar to the Russian Cossacks. Gabaldon (1897) finds it not unlike the English Jig. The woman carries her arms nearly vertical, while the man keeps his raised, both using castanets. When the dance is executed on the flat foot it is called Charrada Asentado; when on the half-toe, Charrada Saltada, or Picada. It is not unlikely that the Charrada is an off-shoot of the Seguidillas. It is also danced with the couple facing each other and, like the Seguidillas, is not marked with the turns which grace the Jota and the Fandango.

Also of the charros' repertoire is La Rosca, or El Bollo (a twisted cake), which figures at weddings and fiestas. The whole dance is performed around the festive table. To begin, a man executes a bright solo called the "escuadra." Then a lady joins him and together they dance the Charrada, the man pursuing his partner who adroitly keeps the table always between them.

A dance with an original if oafish note is the *Zandango* of Valladolid, which in Zamora changes its name to Pancha Corra. In it the dancers form two lines, men in one line, women in the other moving forward and back to the sound of castanets. Executing a half-turn, they approach each other backwards until they bump violently into

[1] Aurelio Capmany, "Folklore y Costumbres de España," Vol. II (El Baile y La Danza), Casa Editorial, Alberto Martin, 1934, Barcelona.

[2] Fuertes y Piqueras, Mariano Soriano, "Music Arabe-Española," J. Oliveres, impresor de S. M., 1853, Barcelona.

Photo by Valente

COSTUMES OF CASTILE—
PILAR LOPEZ, ARGENTINITA and FEDERICO REY

Argentinita, a pure Castilian herself, and her sister, Pilar Lopez, in their richly ornamented native costumes pantomime with grace and coquetry the boy-meets-girl sketch with Federico Rey as their partner.

one another! The girls are so expert at this that there is no man whom they do not succeed in throwing off-balance. This trick has been noted in the Gallegada of Galicia. The Salamancans also dance the Boleras de los Gallegos changing the name to Boleras de Sequeros.

In Largartera (Toledo) the *Baile de la Manzana* is more of a ceremony than a dance-choreography. It is part of wedding festivities, and consists of the young bride dancing with every man, young or old, who deposits a coin in the center of an apple which she offers. Since not to ask her would be an unpardonable offense, and since not to accept would be unthinkable, the poor girl often dances so unceasingly that she becomes ill. She dances holding the apple impaled on a knife and should the money fall out it is reclaimed by the man. This necessitates her moving very rigidly and holding the apple above her head. El Baile de la Manzana was first written of in 1555 by Sebastian de Horozco. Surely its origin is of great antiquity. It seems a part of some pagan ritual, for it recalls the custom prevalent in Tarragona of giving to all the men present at a baptism an apple and a bunch of flowers, representing respectively original sin and paradise.

In Avila, *La Dulzaina* is popular. This jota-like dance is the couple movement from the Boleras de los Gallegos, which was once very popular in Castile. Variations on the Dulzaina are La Cinta in which the girl throws a ribbon on the floor and the boy must pick it up and tie it around his waist without losing the beat of his technically difficult steps; or La Peseta in which a peseta serves the same, if less difficult, role as the ribbon in La Cinta.

In Cuenca, at the Fiesta de las Majas, a prize is given to the prettiest girl seen dancing the Seguidillas.

Of Leon is *El Bailao*, which is an adaptation of the Charrada: and the Giraldilla, which is much like that of Asturia, but danced "a lo alto" (aristocratically). Wedding dances of Leon include the Baile Corredo, a slow, stately couple dance; the Dulzaina in a double circle; the Entradillo, in which the men begin with very fancy solos, after which the girls choose their partners from among the soloists, and all dance together; and lastly, the Corro in which the men dance while the women walk around them in a large circle playing their castanets.

Of Burgos is the *Agudillo* or the Agudo which resembles very much the Seguidillas (which it is sometimes called) save that the woman dances without the coquetry apparent in the Seguidillas, but with her eyes cast down modestly a lo alto, while the man performs at breath-taking speed. (This dance is called by a variety of names; A lo Ligero, Pasan, Milan, Brincandillas, Arriba, A la Pandera, Al Pandero, A lo Alto.) A lo Pecado (also called A lo Grave, A lo Llano,

Photo by Stadler

COSTUME OF SALAMANCA—ARGENTINITA

Photo by D'Ora, Paris

COSTUME OF LAGARTERA—ARGENTINITA

A lo Bajo, Al Paran or Parilla, Jotilla or Jota) has much the same structure as the Agudillo, save that the tempe is slower and the character more grave. During Lent when the girls of Burgos must dance together, since mixed dancing is prohibited, they skip and sing the Ruedas in a circle.

In all parts of the province of Segovia the popular dance resembles the majority of those in Old Castile. An old round dance executed in a double circle to the simple step of step side (R)— together (L)—Step side (R) with half-turn—point (L), of Segovia introduces the "cut-in"; to seek a partner, a man has only to approach a dancing couple, remove his hat and the lady leaves her partner to dance with him. The Seguidillas appears (according to Felipe Pedrell) under the name Habas Verdes (green beans) and is very popular in Salamanca. The "montaracias" (mountaineers) dance it at fiestas known as "herredores."

THE LEVANTINE. The Levantine, which includes Valencia and Murcia, because of the strong influence of Greek culture together with that of Carthage and Rome, has a style and character differing distinctly from that of other regions of Spain. There is a gentle aristocracy of movement coupled with gaiety, a certain sophistication in the naïveté, which comes only to those races which have behind them many centuries of culture. All the dances of the Levantine show this style of movement and interpretation. The Levantines are a happy people, loving life and the flowers and music of life. Perhaps the Greeks left them a strain of philosophy and the Arabs a taste for color, for their costumes are among the loveliest of Spain and recall those worn by the modern Greeks and Balkans.

The *Jota Valenciana*, sometimes called la Danza de los Huertanos, is the most popular dance of Valencia. It is danced in couples on the plaza, the dancers using castanets; the girls wear heeled shoes and the boys, alpargatas (rope-soled sandals). The Jota is an elegant dance, something like the Bolero and is performed asentao. It is not so energetic as the northern dances nor so gentle and alluring as the Andalucian, but it is merry and gracious in character. As early as the 17th century the Jota or (Danza) was used to celebrate the bringing of the archives into Tarragona, and again in 1762 at the laying of the cornerstone of the Cathedral of Lerida. It is even danced at the funeral of infants to show joy that the pure little soul is again "con los angeles" (with the angels). *La Valenciana* differs little from the Jota Valenciana.

In Bocairente (Jativa, Albarda and Oteniente) the *Danza* is called danseas, and although the steps and style remain essentially the same,

Photo by Valente

COSTUMES OF THE LEVANTINE—
PILAR LOPEZ, ARGENTINITA, and FEDERICO REY

it is performed in a sort of wheel formation. Another form of the
Danza existing in Bocairente is performed on the feast day of St.
Augustine. The large bonfire in the center of the dancing circle may
date back as far as the Phoenicians, since they too danced around
fires, although the music, according to Inzenga, cannot be very old.
The dance is serious and decorous, danced in couples with castanets.

The *Xaquera Vella* or (aquiera villa) is so dignified and elegant
that it recalls the Pavane of the 17th century. It is performed in
couples facing each other in two long lines, dancing with gravity and
modesty the courtship motif which figures in all couple dances.
Inzenga y Castellanos claims that, according to the accompanying
music, this dance is one of the oldest of Spain. "The dance in its en-
tirety is as simple and chaste as it is charming and elegant. The couples
approach and withdraw from one another with various movements as
though symbolizing the conflict between daring and modesty...
crossing each other in partial wheels, chains and other attractive
figures... subdued into ceremonial salutations suited to the feigned
state of being in love... the final one (figure) consists in the woman
turning on herself while the man holds her raised hand, after which
he retains it and deposits thereon a furtive and respectful kiss."
Adulterations of the Xaquera Vella are the Ball de Torrent and the
Ball de Moixent. The Copeo is also of Bocairente, and is supposed to
have come originally from Mallorca. It is a lively couple dance with
some zapateo ornamenting its 6/8 rhythm.

The Tarara is the dance of lower Maestrazgo, having been im-
ported from Castile, and retaining the Castilian coplas which accompany it. Other couple dances, stemming from the Jota are Las
Pandaretes, El Furioso and La Rapsodia.

In Alicante the Danza is much like the Fandango, but has movement of a slower tempe; and Albaida favors the festival street-dance
called Las Folias.

Castellon de la Plana boasts of several popular dances. Foremost
among these is the Bolangera which is similar to that of Catalunya.
It is danced by four couples, and is said to have originated in the old
brandas or ruedas (wheel or round dances). But this dance is staid
and monotonous, and at the end of the fiesta the Castellanos dance
the Arenilla (little spider). This is a couple dance in which the boy
tries to step on the feet of the girl, the spectators shout encouragement, teasing and urging the dancers on.

All through the Levantine one finds circular dances of dignified and
ritualistic character, which most surely date back to the Greek occupation.

Murcia, "the garden of Spain," retains much of the flavor of the

Moor in both customs and popular songs. But the dances which go with these minor half-oriental songs are gay and lively, and yet, like the Valencian, possess a certain sophisticated dignity. At one time the *Parranda* was the most popular dance of Murcia. To Seguidillas tempe, it was a round dance which involved a change of partners between coplas. "At the end of the copla the dance is suspended, and the lines approach one another so that the boy can talk to his partner. . . . These pauses for amorous conversation are the most interesting part of the dance. They are more or less long according to the whim of the musician. . . . With the second copla the boy passes behind the girl at his side, both advancing one pace, to place himself in front of a new partner with whom he will dance and converse until the following copla. . . . If a boy wants to have a longer conversation with his favorite girl. . . . He tries to influence the musician, who is the arbitrary judge in this matter." [3]

The Pardica of Moratalla is very like the Parranda.

La Huertana, sometimes called Las Murcianas, is more difficult of execution than the Parranda and so is more popular with the folk. It is to a Malagueña tempe, and features a *vuelta sobresut*. Sometimes accompanied by tambourine, it can become a very acrobatic show-off piece for the man.

The Zangano is another lively dance which is choreographically original in that it is danced by two women and a man and is based on a theme of flirtatious pantomime.

From Andalucia the Murcianos have borrowed the Fandanguillo and the Malagueña, making it their own only in style of interpretation.

EXTREMADURA. Extremadura, a region little known outside of Spain, lies along the Portuguese border, and reveals in its folk music the long years of Moslem domination. Although the Extremadurans are not, some writers claim, given to dancing, their most popular dance is *La Chacona* (called also Ratrojo or Villano) and is of Basque origin. It is a mild couple dance, far less exciting than the Jota Extremeña, sometimes called the Fandanguillo. The spirited movements of the dance, which much resembles the Castilian Fandango, are set off by the use of castanets and tambourine. The Habas Verdes of Salamanca is also popular in Extremadura, as is the Baile de la Manzana of neighboring Toledo, here called Los Ramose. Rafael Monge has written an interesting account of the wedding ceremonies which feature Los Ramose. "After having obtained the paternal consent,

---

[3] Inzenga y Castillanos, "Bailes y Cantos Populares de España," A. Romero A., 1888, Madrid.

the "ajamayos" and "ajamayas" are named. These are the parents of the bride and groom, or their most intimate friends. The day before the wedding, the bride and her two "ajamayas" dedicate themselves to cleaning and adorning the bridal chamber. They adorn the bed with ribbons, rosettes and embroidered linens. Then they suspend from the head of the bed a hand-towel, given by the groom, lace-edged, ribbon-trimmed, and embroidered with mottos of San Benito. That evening all the young men of the village go to the house of the bride to sing coplas alluding to her future happiness, while her family occupy themselves with preparing the wedding feast. The next morning the bridal couple repair to the church to confess and communicate; later come those invited. After the wedding ceremony, the bride retires with her "ajamayas" to put on her costume de gala, as does likewise the groom. . . . All the party dressed in their best, they dance Seguidillas to the sound of panderos, and, when night falls, everyone goes to the door of the bride's house to dance "Los Ramose"—a dance in which the groom offers his consort half a potato or an apple stuck on the point of a knife, and which has inside it a duro or more money according to the financial possibilities of the donor." [4]

[4] Quoted from Isobel de Palencia "El Traje Regional de España," B. T. Batsford, Ltd., 1926, London.

Chapter

VI

R E G I O N A L (South)

*T*he home of Spanish dancing," say the Kinneys, "is south of the
latitude of Madrid in the flowery region where the caliphs ruled.
Where falls the shadow of a castle of the Moors, on that soil blooms
the dance." Today the Andalucian girls, descendants of the gaditanes
who set Rome by the ears, are all, as Cervantes puts it, "born to
dance." They have "honey in their hips."

The Spanish dance, long an art in Cadiz, was much suited to the
Andalucian temperament. Greatly enriched during the occupation of
the Moors, it blossomed in the passionate south until it soon became
the joy of life and the reason thereof. Even the Church incorporated
dancing into its ritual, this form of worship being still used in the
Cathedral of Sevilla by the choir boys. And who has not read of the
celebrations of the Cruz de Mayo, when every patio is open to
the street, the cross itself decorated in lights and flowers, while am-
bulant dancers of every class whirl from house to house?

What is not always understood, however, is that the Andalucians
have spontaneously created an art in the very execution of the folk
dance. They dance for their partners, but perform air designs for
the audience that are without equal in the world; they dance for their
partners, but captivate their audience completely; they dance for sheer
enthusiasm, yet execute a choreographic design that puts to shame
many professional choreographers; they dance for sheer enthusiasm,
yet achieve a rhythmic counterpoint that challenges the best musicians; they have created a dance in the village square in alpargatas,
and themselves refined it to a theater art in their own patios!

Courtesy the Hispanic Society of America

"Sevilla, The Dance" by Sorolla y Bastida, 1863-1923

"What is loosely called Spanish dancing was really the art of this one province, (Andalucia) the Roman Betica, El Andaluz of the Moors." [1]

Most typical of Andalucian dances (and most difficult) is the *Sevillanas*. We know that it is an outgrowth of the Seguidillas Manchegas of Castile. Harold Bauer calls the Sevillanas, "the proudest dance I know."

"The Sevillanas is the dance of gaiety, the dance of the laughing castañuelas (castanets), the soul of Andalucia, the land of which they say, 'After Andalucia there can be only Paradise ... but with a little hole in Paradise through which one can peep at Andalucia!' " [2]

Like all folk dances the Sevillanas is subject in detail of step and gesture to the technical skill of the performer, but the frame-work is invariably the same. It consists of seven coplas, but often only three or five are used. Each copla is divided into three parts, each of these consisting of twelve bars of music; each part begins with the step, *sevillanas*, and ends with a pass. The dance is for one or two couples, but has been adapted for everything from solo to group. It is performed with castanets, and the use of these as well as the steps themselves are in counter-time, making the whole affair extremely difficult.

Otero says that the dancer who masters the Sevillanas will find absurdly easy any other dance of Spain. Line and counter-line in the limbs of the performers lend a bewildering grace. At the end of each copla the dancers stop suddenly in statuesque immobility. It is an art to bring oneself into a perfect pose here, and if one succeeds there is the reward of "Bien parado!" from the spectators.

The old Sevillanas Boleras, though built on the same choreographic base as the Seguidillas Sevillanas used elevation and *batterié, cuartas* and *voladas,* necessitating the use of a quick foot in a light shoe. The Seguidillas Sevillanas depends more on body-line and the spiraled pass which closes each section of each copla.

Martinez says the Sevillanas together with the Panaderos, Peteneras, Jaleo, are derived from the *Cachucha* of Andalucia. There is little direct choreographic information to be had about the Cachucha itself, now that a century has passed since it was popular in Spain. "A lady visiting Malaga, at the beginning of the last century, assures us that the dancing in Malaga is the most expressive, its songs the most melodious, its costumes the most elegant. There she saw the Cachucha; a dance considered by some, lascivious and indecent." [3]

[1] Cyril Rice, "Dancing in Spain," British Continental Press, 1931, London.
[2] Paul Reboux, "Teresina," Souvenir Program.
[3] Carl van Vechten, "The Music of Spain," Alfred A. Knopf, 1918, New York.

TRAJE CORTO—JOSÉ GRECO

"Mr. Philip Hale points out the fact that the Bolero and the Cachucha (which by the way one seldom hears of nowadays) were the popular Spanish dances when Mesdames Faviani and Fanny Elssler visited Paris." [4]

The Sevillanas, "most famous of Andalucian dances," was first danced as a solo by La Campanera in the cafés of Sevilla, to the great delight of the habitués. It became at once a favorite and proved the vehicle to popularity of the two dancers, Guerro and Carmencita. It is a dance of changing moods and lyric emotion. The performers though dancing only for themselves, smiling only for each other, yet play upon the heartstrings of the watcher until, caught up by the pulsing rhythm, he shouts, "Que Dios bendiga tu madre!"

Many other Andalucian dances grew from the Seguidillas Sevillanas. The *Peteneras* has long been known among the gitanos both as song and dance. The name is said to have come from a celebrated singer of flamenco who lived over a century ago. Popular in the province of Cadiz (possibly since the days of the gaditanes) it migrated to Cuba and returned with a strong Negro flavor in the rhythm. It made its formal appearance in 1894 at a fiesta Andaluz, performed by Don Paulino Ruiz. The three coplas of the Peteneras were at once acclaimed in cafetin and patio. Shortly thereafter, Otero and Segura set the elusive steps of the Peteneras into a routine.

Las Manchegas, as danced in Andalucia, is quite different from the dance of Castile which bears the same name—for whatever the Andalucian touches he transforms! After a complicated "salida," the three coplas are danced at twice the speed of the Sevillanas and the steps are laced with the beautiful *pasada de Sevillanas*. Otero says it is, "not a gracious dance, but a rapid dance, difficult in the footwork."

At the close of the last century, Busquets called the intoxicating *Bolero* the national dance of Spain, and the most popular dance in Andalucia. But it has already passed into the realm of the classic school dance, superseded by the Sevillanas.

El Olé is said to be of ancient origin, but was recreated by Carmen la Cigarrera, in about 1840. It is a simple dance technically, set in two coplas, and relying entirely on the elegance and grace of the performer (which must be a woman) and savors much of the classical Bolero; *pas de buret* and *lazos*, mingling with the *pasos de vascos*, and *encajes*. By 1850 the fame of a Sevillian dancer was judged by her performance of the Olé. Carl van Vechten identifies the Olé as a Polo Gitano. Havelock Ellis says it is a corruption of the Sarabande.

[4] *Ibid.*

Six Action Shots by Dwight Godwin

SEGUIDILLAS SEVILLANAS—
LA MERI and PIETRO DI FALCO
a. SEVILLANAS, the first step of the first copla

b. Panaderos, the closing step of the first copla

c. ESPLANTES, the closing step of the second copla

d. Llamadas, the first section of the third copla

e. Passadas, the closing step of the third copla

f. "Bien Parado!"

"The so-called gypsy dances of Spain are Spanish dances which the Spaniards are tending to relinquish, but which the gypsies have taken up with energy and skill." "The Spaniard may be troubled by the thought that he is behind the times, but the Spanish gypsy is not. . . . He asks nothing better than to spend his days and nights in dancing and singing." [5] It is very possible that the Andalucian Olé is the old Olé Gaditane, vicariously preserved by the gypsies.

Los Panaderos dates, according to some authorities as far back as the Fandango, having come out of Cadiz. Originated—or preserved, who knows which—by the gypsies, it was first spontaneously sung and danced in the streets. Before 1870, the Panaderos, Fandango and Bolero were immensely popular, and after an evening's entertainment, artist and folk alike would "van a pasar un rato en las Cruces de Mayo, en donde era indispensible bailar pasadas de sevillanas, panaderos, fandangos, boleras, etc." [6]

Panaderos, Olé and Vito are all considered flamenco dances of the Bulerias type.

The salida of Los Panaderos is a stately step that recalls the Pavane. But then the couple execute a *vuelta*, and are off into an Andalucian rhythm whose speed calls for two *pasos de sevillanas* to a bar—twice the ordinary speed of that step.

El Vito, first a flamenco song and used as a background for *zarandeo* by the gypsies, appeared in the streets of Sevilla as a popular dance toward the early part of the last century. By 1840 it had attained to the cafetins and found its best protagonist in Maria Cazuela, gitana "de cuatro costados" (on four sides) . . . "fea y contrahecha" (ugly and misformed) . . . but apparently quite an artist. The Vito is for a woman alone, and is a parody of a bullfight, which pantomime quality alone should show its gypsy origin.

La Malagueñas originated in Malaga. As a folk dance it is similar to the Sevillanas in that it is danced in coplas, though of slightly different length than those of the Sevillian dance. Performed in alpargatas by the folk, it has a variety of foot-work of the bouncy type. Gautier describes a Malagueña which he calls the "danse locale de Malaga." This seems to be the same school dance described by the Kinneys in "The Dance." (The flamenco songs called Malagueñas are slow and sensuous and have nothing in common with the folk dance save the name.)

There are many other Andalucian dances: La Jerzana, Las Guajiras, Las Molleras, El Fandanguillo, El Jaleo. They are, generally, only provincial interpretations of the Queen of Dances, Las Sevillanas.

[5] Irving Brown, "Deep Song," Harper Bros., 1929, New York.
[6] José Otero "Tratado de Bailes," Guia Oficial, 1912, Sevilla.

Photo by Bruno of Hollywood

ARGENTINITA, PILAR LOPEZ in "Traje Corto"

In a region such as Andalucia where dancing is a part of everyday life, where half the population "contemplate the zapateado," while the other half creates it, it is not surprising that it is difficult to draw a clear distinction between the "folk dance," the "gypsy dance," the "school dance" and the "theater dance." Doubtless in another generation it will be just as difficult to classify the neo-classic or renaissance dance, although now there are teachers of the old school, such as Juan Beaucaire-Montalvo, who disapprove of dancing the "filigree" dances to music of Spain's classic composers, as much as Otero, twenty years ago, deplored the passing of the *lazos* and *cuartas* from the Sevillanas.

A folk dance is a dance created by the folk . . . and, assumedly, danced by them. But in Andalucia the folk are artists; what one dances in the street another sees and immediately betters, and before a month is gone the dance may have completely changed its steps. Not yet content, the masters of dance, with this wealth of material before them, and caught by the immediate popularity of a rhythm, a title, a dance, start to routine the spontaneous steps. They are hardly well begun on this work when the girls of cigarette factory and "merceria" (notions shop) are knocking at their doors to be taught the latest steps; and before you can say Jack Robinson the local dancers have lifted last month's street dance onto the stage! It is no wonder that historians of the past and pilgrims of the present heartily disagree about practically everything except the Sevillanas.

Let us make an analogy. Suppose we suppressed all the clocks in New York so that no one knew or cared what time it was. Suppose we made it eternally spring, so that sidewalk cafés would bloom, and people take siestas in the afternoon. Suppose we moved redolent sections of Georgia and Louisiana to Broadway, and everyone began to listen all day to the blues and boogie of the negro. Suppose everyone suddenly felt sixteen. We will not change the dancing schools and the theater, for that is a very necessary part of the picture. Have you followed the analogy? Can you imagine what would happen? We would never know who invented what, nor when and where what dance began and another ended, nor the exact temporal relationship between music and dance. I am rather inclined to believe we wouldn't care, either, but would just let the foreigners seek *us* out and try to discover the this from the that; for *we'd* be creating a dance-art as the Andalucian has, which is surely infinitely more fun than studying about it!

It is seldom possible to transplant the folk dance "as is" to the stage. There are, of course, notable exceptions to this rule. But generally the dance, exactly as you see it done in the open square, would

Photo by Valente

"CAFÉ DE CHINITAS"; choreographic "BOSQUEJO" by ARGENTINITA—
ARGENTINITA, PILAR LOPEZ, JOSÉ GRECO

be singularly lacking in interest performed for a theater public. Yet many are the authentic folk dances presented and applauded. This is because these dances have been adapted. Nearly every Spanish dancer has one or two folk dances in her repertoire.

There are several ways to set about arranging any folk dance for theater consumption. To begin with, one tries to execute these dances not as the folk would do them but as folk would desire to do them. That is, the basic quality and character must remain untouched, but the actual execution must be lighter and freer than is generally found among the farmer folk who dance of a Sunday. I do not mean that the step must be changed to attain this, but, the steps must be more clearly enunciated. I do not believe you will find in the whole of Aragon a dancer as dainty and light as Argentinita, yet the Aragonesa will execute the same steps with the same style, envying her only her execution.

Secondly, one must select the best steps of the repertoire and weave them into a dance. Generally, in each community, there are a handful of dancers who have real talent. Each of these has one or two variations which he does on the basic steps and for which he is applauded and admired in the village. You should dance like all the best dancers in the province rolled into one.

Thirdly, the dance must be choreographed. Normally, these folk dances last all day. They are done to amuse the dancers not the watchers. Obviously, you cannot, alone, dance the Jota all day and expect your audience and yourself to hold out. On the typical music, then, you must set a varied and well-balanced routine of the typical steps which will give the audience a synthesis of the folk dance you are portraying.

Many of the folk dances are so limited, from a theater viewpoint, in variety of step, that it is nearly impossible to arrange them into theatrical form. Yet the spirit, the costume and the music are too charming to let alone! To underline the characterization, then, a sequence of pantomime is used. This has always been the custom of Spanish choreographers. Otero presents the Gallegada with a few bars of coy, gauche pantomime passages.

Argentinita carried this pantomime custom to a much higher point than it had ever before achieved. She handled the communal dance delightfully, almost always working in a gentle sketch of "boy-meets-girl," accenting the character of the folk themselves while doing so. One suspects that when she treated a dance, poor in actual steps, she borrowed from the next door province to give brilliance to the whole, which one can be quite sure the natives do themselves now and then.

Chapter

VII

F L A M E N C O

*T*here has been a good deal of speculation anent the racial origins which have gone into the making of the amazing flamencos of Spain. The wandering people which the world knows as gypsies are, most probably, from India. Springing from the caste of Sudras, they are still possessors of a pride which has done much toward lifting their dance and song to the level of an art, in the eyes of a skeptical world. The earliest migrations of these people are recorded in old Persian chronicles, and there is written testimony to their presence in Egypt and Palestine before the Christian era. Even then they were expert metal workers. Homer writes that they were "beloved by Vulcan because of their skill at the forge." It was this skill which prompted Alexander in 400 B.C. to send many of them from India into Macedonia. Much of the Cale language (some authorities say one-third) consists of Sanskrit words.

These Sudras in their wanderings, mixed with both the Phoenician and the Egyptian, although it can be assumed that even then it was only their code of racial purity, based on that pride which set them "above all nations—a race of kings and queens—" which prevented their complete absorption by the peoples into whose lands they migrated. Moving west over Europe, the gypsies met everywhere with the worst possible treatment. All manner of crimes were laid at their doors, and laws and individuals forever drove them forth. Who knows to what remote Indian philosophy of life they owe their very existence?

The Moors who conquered Andalucia were made up of three dif-

77

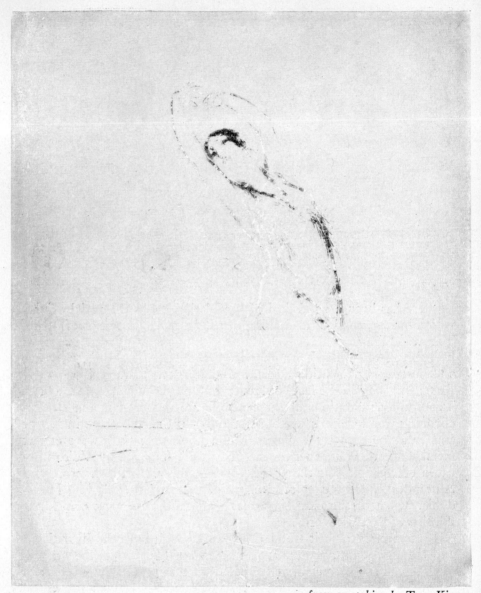

from an etching by Troy Kinney

"PASTORA IMPERIO"

ferent peoples; the Berbers, who are of white complexion and whose origin might even be Basque; the Almohades, great warriors, but with no interest in art or culture; the Yemenite Arabs who brought with them a highly-developed culture. The Berbers and Almohades eventually grew jealous of the Arabs and united to overthrow the Caliphate at the end of the 9th century. This left the Yemenites only the kingdom of Sevilla—which city until today enjoys a prestige doubtless due to the longer influence of a fine culture.

After the fall of Granada things went badly for the gypsies. They had found in the Moor a spiritual kinship which encouraged them to freely intermarry. The Andalucian gypsy, then, is a mixture of Arab and Indian. But as late as 1417, the Sudra gypsies were still arriving in Barcelona; and, to this day there is a definite differentiation drawn between Catalunian and Andalucian gitanos. (Carmen Amaya is of the Catalunian tribe.)

In 1499, there was a decree issued that gypsies—still oppressed and hounded—should settle down and cease wandering, a certain protection being offered. Many gypsies did so, and these were called "Castellanos Nuevos" in opprobrium by those "Gitanos Bravíos," who refused to relinquish their birthright of the open road.

At the end of the 18th century, Charles III improved the laws which discriminated against the gypsies; and, thus encouraged, these people came down at last out of their hiding places. But they were noisy—sang and danced at odd hours when conservative folk slept— and gradually they were left alone in their barrios which were called "gitanerias" (from gitano) or "cañadas" (from cañi).

Today there are forty-thousand-odd gypsies in Spain. A century ago they were still an outcast people, only a few poets and pilgrims delighting in their wit, their passion and their songs. But now a veritable cult of flamencoism has sprung up, and the Sudras have come into their own.

Some authorities believe that the gitanos and flamencos are direct descendants of the Moors, a belief which at least the gitanos of Granada are inclined to accept. But there are others who maintain that they are not a residue of the Moors, but members of the race migrating from India. De Falla,[1] sustaining this theory, yet finds the Moors have first influence on the flamenco music. Havelock Ellis suggests that the name of "gypsy" might have been applied because of the racial proficiency in dances of the Egyptian type, and the dancing of Cadiz in gaditanian days, comes definitely under that heading.

The title "flamenco" is of uncertain origin. Various theories have been put forward. Blas Infante believes the word derives from the

[1] Manuel De Falla, famous composer, 1876-1946.

Arabic "felah mengu" which means "peasant in flight," for many Spaniards thought the gypsies were descendants of the expelled Moors. Generally accepted among Spanish dancers, to whom I have talked, is the theory that the Spanish mercenary soldiers on their return from the low countries drank and sang so much in the taverns that noisy public behavior came to be called "flamenco." Afterwards, all noisy behavior was called flamenco, and soon the term was applied only to the noisy, singing gypsy. Cyril Rice writes, "This term 'flamenco,' first noted in 1871, is one whose history has provided Spanish philologists with many hours of pleasant, but inconclusive, research."

Some claim the gypsy has no song and dance of his own, but adopts and colors the arts of the country to which he migrates. Bercovici says that one exception to this rule is the dance called "Tañana" which is based on zarandeo, and is common to gypsies all over the world. But the gypsies of Spain sing and dance like the gypsies of Moscow; and the Romanos from Macedonia can join the Flamenco circle without loss of tempe or style. "Django, the famous French gypsy... after hearing an alegrias played by Carlos Montoyo, returned to the zone in Clichy and played alegrias in a cuadro Flamenco of Andalucian gypsies." [2]

But the Flamenco dance is no set thing to have been borrowed from another people; it is a racial mode of expression. Argentinita says that "the gypsies have rhythm in their veins instead of blood like the rest of humanity."

The largest gypsy barrios in Spain are la Triana in Sevilla and el Albaicin in Granada. Triana has been so-called since the 13th century and thanks to the still-observed law of Al Mu-tamid requiring all the inhabitants to whitewash their dwellings at regular intervals, the quarter is still one of the loveliest in the lovely city of Sevilla.

In Albaicin cuevas are the homes of the gitanos. But caves large and whitewashed inside and out; caves whose front doors are so built that each looks like a small, white geranium-starred adobe house; caves which have at least two rooms, with an altar to the Virgin, and copper pots and pans on every wall.

In Granada the gypsies are called "Gitanos"; in Sevilla, "Flamencos," but the terms are relatively interchangeable. There are two main tribes of gypsies, the Maya and the Amalla. They claim to be very rigid in their custom of not marrying outside their tribe. But marriage customs, though strict, are unorthodox; divorce consisting in just up and leaving the husband's house. Walter Starkie writes:

"Pedro de Castellón then proceeded to give me a severe moral

2 Donald Duff, "Flamenco," Modern Music, May-June, 1940.

Photo by Paul Hanson

"Los Cales"—Thaia Mara and Arthur Mahoney

FLAMENCA OF TRIANA—PILAR LOPEZ

lecture upon the *lacha ye trupos* (corporeal chastity) of the Gypsy race in Spain which reminded me of what George Borrow says on that subject in *The Zincali*.[3]

" 'Not one of those women you see in this camp,' said Don Pedro, 'would look at a man who did not belong to the tribe. From the earliest age they have been brought up to consider lacha ye trupos as their most precious possession. Why, every young girl dreams of the day when she is led in the marriage procession, and her white *dicló*, the proof of her maidenhood, floats in the air.'

" 'Yes, *plaloró*,' murmured I softly. 'I remember how the Gypsy *copla* says:

" ' "En un praíto berde
Tendí mi pañuelo;
Como salieron, mare, tres rositas
Como tres luseros." ' "

" 'That is true,' continued the chief. 'The whole tribe must be sure that the bride is a virgin, for that is the most precious patrimony she can bring her husband. And after the marriage, do not imagine that he will relax his vigilance. A Gypsy husband knows the thoughts of his wife and woe betide her if she plays any tricks upon him.'

" 'What happens, Don Pedro,' said I, 'if a wife is unfaithful to her husband? Is there any secret tribunal of Gypsies which will try her and condemn her? Is there no divorce ceremony among the Gypsies of Spain?'

" 'Divorce indeed, brother! What would we be doing with divorce? We do not need any secret tribunal to try our wives when they are unfaithful. We ourselves act as judge and executioner. But the occasion rarely arises, brother, for every *romi* knows that her *rom's* eye is swifter and sterner than the wolf's." [4]

"The frequency of unions between Gypsy and Spaniard, and the standard of chastity prevalent among the girls, have been much debated; among the most enthusiastic investigators having been the aforesaid representative of the Bible Society, George Borrow, who arrived at conclusions highly satisfactory to the champions of Romani morality. Prosper Mérimée, who considered he was better able to conduct such researches than a person of semi-ecclesiastical position, hints that he did not find their virtue so inexpugnable. This interesting question is not of purely academic moment, but has also some bearing on certain aspects of gypsy dancing." [5]

[3] G. Borrow, *The Zincali*, London, 1841. P. 267.
[4] (The above quote is from: Spanish Raggle-Taggle by Walter Starkie, London, John Murray, Albermarle Street, W., November 1934, P. 277, 278.)
[5] Cyril Rice, "Dancing in Spain," British Continental Press, 1931, London.

BAILE FLAMENCO—JUAN MARTINEZ and ANTONITA

The Flamenco dance was born of an oriental people, and in the orient the dance is never a pastime but always a ceremonial. To the Spanish gypsy it is something even more. It is a declaration of independence, the national hymn of a fast disappearing race without a country. This is why they are so jealous of it and reveal it to so few. "Just as in the 13th century the kingdom of Granada formed a tiny and pathetic fragment of the departed glories of the Western Caliphate, so again today does it figure as the last stronghold of a fading tradition." [6]

Now the gypsy dances as the result of a mood which grips him. Obviously it is nearly impossible for an artist who must appear night after night, no matter what his mood, to transplant this dance in its pure form to the stage. It is told that a gitana once said to a great Spanish actress, "You 'comicos' don't know what we artists feel!" [7] The gypsy himself, in his own cueva rarely really dances under alien eyes. In his dance he offers up some thing of his own soul to a Supreme Being—and one does not perform rituals before an unbeliever.

If you are a tourist in Spain and you desire to see the flamenco dance you will go, perhaps, first to Granada. But you are dealing with Arab blood and the Arabs know how to entice the buyer and drive a hard bargain. Presently you will manage to have it "especially arranged." When you are at last in the cave, you will find a half dozen girls gazing at you with brooding eyes. A guitarist strums idly. La Capitaz gives a signal and girls rise and go through the steps of one or two dances. There is no spirit, no fire, no interest in the affair at all! If you sit quietly, at the end of ten minutes you will be allowed to give them twenty-five American dollars and go away. But you will not have seen gitano dancing.

Then, perhaps, you will go to Sevilla. Here the Cuadro Flamenco is a feature of nearly any cafetin. It consists of one or two guitarists, several women dancers and one or two male dancers. These sit in a semicircle on the small stage. One at a time they rise to perform, while those seated make the jaleo—the combination of palmadas, taconeo, and shouts of encouragement. But some of the girls will dance for the audience, smirking a little; some will be entirely bored; while others will introduce all sorts of alien variations, such as castanets, squat-flings, back-bends and high kicks. For this art is born of a folk, and that very folk, being ignorant, are unaware of the importance of artistic integrity.

So, if you are a tourist, however much you may have enjoyed it,

[6] André Levinson, "Argentina," Editions des Chroniques du Jour, 1928, Paris.
[7] Argentinita in a lecture on the Spanish Dance.

TRAJE DI COLA—NILA AMPORE

it is extremely doubtful if you will see real flamenco dancing in Sevilla either.

Only if you can go to the cuevas accompanied by some one the gypsies know as their friend, only after you have gone often and bought them much "manzanilla" (wine), only then will they warm a little towards you. And then perhaps one evening they will forget you are there—and they will really dance!

That is one way to see the true Flamenco dance. The other is to stay long in Andalucia, and to become a tireless habitué of the cafés where the cuadro Flamenco is seen. If you watch patiently and long, on a certain night one of the performers, for a personal reason or for something outside himself, will be gripped by strong emotion and he will forget his audience and lose himself in the dance. Then you will see the flamenco dance! You will see, too, an apparently hitherto sane public of Spaniards going quite mad with excitement!

As in the corrida the sequence in which the artists appear in the cuadro is determined by age, the youngest appears first, the oldest, last. And since the oriental assumes that it is experience which makes an artist, this system also produces the "good theater" of mounting excitement. A typical cuadro Flamenco might run as follows: a woman dancer opens with a tango; then follows another woman in a Bulerias or Farruca; then a man dancer performs a zapateado; afterwards comes the Alegrias, "queen of dances." The act might close with a Sevillanas by the group, for the flamenco dance is essentially for solo or duet, and group dances must be borrowed from the regional repertoire.

The *Alegrias* is one of the oldest of the gypsy dances; it is the purest, the most refined, the most dignified of the repertoire. Some interpreters suggest "tauramargie" (bullfight) with their movements. The copla which accompanies the dance may be either "alegre" (happy) or sad, but the dance itself, though withdrawn, is not sorrowful, and the music which accompanies the coplas is gay and exhilarating. Alegrias may also be danced "por chufla" (joke). A woman generally dances alegrias in a "traje di cola" (trailed dress), which adds much to the dignity and charm of the movements.

At first the Alegrias was a spontaneous, unformed expression of gypsy joy. Time has given it a certain form. It starts with the "palmas" (hand-claps) in which dancer and guitarist test the tempo; follows an interlude of *paseo* or *filigranos:* then come one or two *desplantes*. These *desplantes* orient guitarist and dancer so that if the two have worked often together they may dispense with them. Then come the *pasos ondulados* which show the grace and elegance of the performer; the six *golpes* and the *desplante* usher in the faster, wilder steps, which are the *pasos con palmadas* and the *taconeo* of the finale. Within this form the dancer can improvise as much as she likes, lengthening each passage to suit her mood of the moment. It is said that Alegrias is never the same twice (which is true of any Flamenco dance) for no dancer ever repeats herself. Most Flamenco dancers execute only one, or at most, two styles of dance and yet have an endless repertoire.

The *Bulerias* is gayer and faster than the Alegrias, though not unlike it in step. It is younger, both actually and in spirit, and is often used as a vehicle to pantomime teasing stories about others. There is a good deal of zarandeo, and apparently some steps taken from the regional dances. Martinez calls it "the cachucha of the gitanos," while Argentinita described it as a Flamenco "jam-session."

The *Farruca* is the "mas cañi de todos," says Carmen de Toledo. It is the first dance which all the children learn, for it embodies all the technique of the other Flamenco dances. Some say it was first introduced by the gitano, Faico. It is "pure dancing, a dance that has no story to unfold, no message to impart, but depends entirely on the proud movements that fascinate the eye, the intricate rhythms that impress themselves upon the ear, all combining in one overwhelming impression of rhythm and force." [8] It is a dance most suited to a man, and when so danced the "caida" (fall) is impressive and exciting, as are the sudden double *vuelta quebradas*. The *zapateo* is strong, the *mediazapato* "stabbing" the floor; the *tiempe di tango*, nearly leaped. It is one of the three Flamenco dances (Tango and Garrotin) in 2/4 time (the majority being in 3/4 and 3/8) and for this reason supposedly influenced, at least musically, by Cuba.

The *Zapateado* is essentially a man's dance. It is composed entirely of *zapateo*, broken only by the occasional use of heel-to-toe movements, or by *vueltas* which slap the heels. The arms are employed scarcely at all, the dancer thrusting his hands into the pockets of his "chaquetilla" (jacket), so as to concentrate on the miracles of *taconeo* which he must perform. "During the early decades of the 19th century the word zapateado became prominent," [9] and since Vuillier states in 1870 that as a flamenco dance it is of relatively recent origin, it may be assumed that it dates from that epoch, although Levinson believes it originated in the 16th century.

The *Garrotin* is originally a couple dance rather in the emotional style of the French Apache dance. The gitano is very rough with his women and here he lets passion sway him. He flings her to the floor, drags her by her hair, shakes her roughly by the wrists, pulls his long "navaje" (knife) from his belt and pursues her with threats. When

[8] Cyril Rice, "Escudero," Souvenir Program.
[9] Rice, *op. cit.*

Photo by Bruno of Hollywood

GARROTIN—JUAN MARTINEZ and ANTONITA

the Garrotin is danced by a woman alone she shakes her hands as though trying to shake off the gitano's rough grip; she clutches her head remembering how he pulled her long hair; she takes her own forefinger in her teeth to show how he pursued her with his knife in his mouth.

The *Tango Flamenco* is originally a woman's dance, though in it she nearly always wears a man's hat. The steps are heavier and simpler than those of the Alegrias or Bulerias, but give more scope for floor-design than the zapateado. Most of the steps are based on the one called *tango*, while the *marianas* is invariably introduced. Tangos may be done "serios y por chufla" (seriously or as a joke). The tango has long been popular in Cadiz, and it is not impossible that it resembles the dance of the gaditanes of Roman times. However, it is sure that its migration to the American colonies greatly enriched it in style and color. It might be well to observe here that the Tango Flamenco has nothing whatever in common with the Argentine tango save the name.

The *Soleares* is a very old gypsy dance. It is not clearly known whether or not it antedates the Alegrias; but these two are said to be the origin of all flamenco dances. They are very similar, both in step and elegance of style, but the alegrias has developed somewhat more taconeo than the soleares. Soleares can also be danced por chufla. The name is said to have come from that of a singer called Soledad, but the mood of sadness and nostalgia which permeates the coplas may be the reason for the title. The soleares, like the garrotin, owes to maestro Otero its popularity as a cafetin dance. The first dancer to perform it outside the "juergas" (parties) wearing the "traje corto" (man's costume), of the flamencos, was La Cuenca, in about 1883.

The *Zambra* has a definitely Moorish origin. We have seen that it was danced at the leilas during the Caliphate of Cordoba. At that time it seems to have been a "courtship" duet, since a certain Moorish potentate offered prizes to "him who could most gracefully dance the zambra with a Moorish maiden." [10] It is claimed that the Moorish zambra exists today in the form of the dance executed in the cathedral of Toledo. Done exclusively by a woman, this is the most Indian of gitano dances.

Most flamenco coplas can be used as dance accompaniment, and so the names of "estilos di canto" (style of singing) become the names of dances. But the dances listed above—alegrias, bulerias, farruca, tango, garrotin, zapateado and zambra—are primarily dances with the

[10] Julian Ribera, "Music in Ancient Arabia and Spain," Stanford University Press, 1929, Calif.

Photo by Annemarie Heinrich, Buenos Aires

ZAMBRA—CARMEN DE TOLEDO

"copla" used only as accompaniment. The soleares is more often sung than danced, but is still recognized as a baile.

Of the flamenco estilos which are more distinctly song than dance, the *Seguidillas Gitano* (seguiriyas gitana) is the most typical. It is composed of four lines as against the seven which go to make up the Spanish Seguidillas. Gypsy songs based on seven lines are called Serranas. This shows that the title of a dance is taken from the title of its song accompaniment (which generally preceded it); and, the title of the song is taken from the poetic form of its lyric. The coplas are improvised as are the dancer's steps. The accompaniment to even the saddest coplas is generally fast, and it is to this rhythm that the dancer "seems to be laughing at the singer's tears." Argentinita says "the gypsies sing their sorrows and dance in a frenzy of gaiety."

The fandanguiyo, the malagueña, and its variations the murciana, tarante, cartageneras, the granadina, the polo (of Granada), the rondeña, tientos, guajiras, and peteneras are rarely danced.

Seatas, "arrows of song" improvised during the Holy Week processionals, and martinetes and carceleras—unaccompanied and improvised in prison—are never danced.

The repertoire of flamenco dances is constantly changing. Those here listed have been popular in this century; but as the 19th century drew to a close, Laura Smith saw danced in the "Puerta del Terra" (gypsy barrio of Cadiz), a song called *Romalis*, which "Tiberius may have seen." She describes it as sung in chorus with softly clapping hands and says it is the gypsy equivalent of the Spanish Olé . . . (Olé Gaditane?).

These are the dances which you will see in the cuadro Flamenco. These are the dances of Alegria. Few have seen any of the ritual dances of which, I feel sure, there may be hundreds. For example, there is the marriage dance—*la danza de casamiento*. On the night of a wedding the entire tribe gathers in a cueva. There is singing and drinking and dancing. But at a certain point in the festivities, the oldest dancer present (she who has taught all the others; she who holds the traditions in her hands) calls a signal, and the entire group begins the dance of casamiento, with the bride and groom dancing together. The music grows wilder and wilder. Suddenly the old woman dancer takes the hand of the bride and leads her into the back room of the cueva (it is walled off only by a curtain). The groom is left dancing alone in the center. He dances his hopes, his fears, his confidence, in that brief five minutes. For suddenly the old dancer runs into the circle waving her hand aloft. On her forefinger she shows the blood of virginity—and the dance takes on a wilder, higher note of joy.

Chapter

VIII

RENAISSANCE

*I*n the past thirty years a new art-form has been born, an art-form which, lacking a title, I have called the renaissance or neo-classic Spanish dance. Three decades ago the Spanish dance had about the same artistic standing as the tap dance. It was the expression of a folk —rhythmic, exciting and fun to watch. There were few who saw its possibilities of growth into an international art-form.

The decadence of the dance in Spain itself began, according to Otero, with the turn of the century. Fifty years ago it was a very necessary adjunct to social life. But the passion for modernity engulfed Spain and she grew ashamed of her dances and of her dancers. The Golden Age of Cerezo's Bolero, when all of Europe clamored for ballets in the Spanish idiom, became a part of history, and Iberia sent forth no dance-ambassador to take the place of Fanny Elssler. Carmencita, Tortajada, Tortola Valencia, Pastora Imperio, Amalia Molina—these had played the world's music halls, but for the general public abroad they were "vaudeville hoofers." Fokine, Massine and other great choreographers had presented Spanish ballets, but these were in the ballet tradition and style with only somewhat distorted bits of Spanish technique superimposed upon them.

The pioneer—some say the creator—of the Spanish renaissance dance was Argentina. The fact that had she failed to do this work it would have inevitably been done by another in the logical evolution of the arts, is beside the point, for no one can take away from her the glory that she it was who forced a skeptical world to respect as a pure art-form the Spanish dance.

"LA ARGENTINA" by PAUL TROUBETZKOY

The solo concert dance was first introduced by Isadora Duncan and Ruth St. Denis. In about 1925 it began to be a popular form, and many dancers, assisted only by a pianist, held the stage alone for the two hours of a complete evening's performance. By the time Argentina made her first world tour (1929), concert dancing was a "fait accompli" for protagonists of ballet, interpretive, modern and even oriental. With the concerts of Argentina, the Spanish dance joined these other forms on the concert stage. Paris and New York saw monthly debuts of ambitious young artists giving full programs in the Iberian techniques. Carola Goya was soon known as the most re-booked dancer in the United States; and Teresina enchanted Paris with her sultry charm.

But the Spanish dance had not only taken a new citadel in the theater world, it had actually borne the flower of a new choreographic style. No more was the dance left to mood and chance, but became a composition which must respect the choreographic triad of floor design, air design and music design, and embody the choreographic rules of contrast. Built as a drama is built, on an emotional scaffold like an inverted "V" of introduction, inciting force of moment, development, climax, denouement, final suspense and final allotment; the mood which inspires the renaissance estilo must be felt only at the first hearing of the music, the first impact of the idea, and then, like the writing of a poem, must be written in the clear memory of that mood. The intentions of the composer must be respected, and the dancer must try to understand and perform that type of dance which the composer intended in his themes. The castanets are not played ad libitum, but are studied out in counter-point like a second voice to the melody. And at the service of all must be a physical and mental knowledge of the technique as complete as is necessary to any great ballet dancer and choreographer combined.

The renaissance Spanish dance moves as an infanta would move—with dignity, with pride—whatever be her other emotions. It uses the vehicle of the Spanish temperament and technique to express moods as varied and deep as any living dance-art. The folk dance was born to amuse the dancer. The cabaret dance was born to amuse the audience. But the classical dance, like Hindu Natya, was born to inspire and to teach. The dance concert, no more than the symphony orchestra concert, is intended for "amusement." Everyone has seen Spanish dancing of one sort or another, but the percentage of those who have understood it is amazingly small, for, unlike the oriental dance, it is too close to us to command the consideration of study. There is a certain form of mental snobbism which respects nothing which it knows or feels. A hero whom one knew at school is no hero.

CAROLA GOYA

And since one has seen Spanish dancing, and rather enjoyed it, it cannot possibly have any artistic value. But this is "le plus ancien et le plus noble des exotismes européens," [1] and if one understands it, one cannot help but respect it whether or not it touches one's heart.

The classic technique of the Spanish dance is composed of the steps of the regional dances and the Flamenco dance. Technique of arms and body is from the same source. All have been depurated without losing character. Technical acquisitions of the ballet of the 18th and 19th centuries have been dropped and are now used only in the presentation of dances of that period. It seems nearly incredible that a folk could create a technique in a repertoire so complete that it stands as classic without the addition of any nobler steps. As a race the Spaniard is the greatest dancer in the world, for no other people have created a complete dance-art in the fields and patios!

The Andalucian popular dance is the unique case in choreographic history where the folk, unaided by outside influences, have themselves created a finished art-form. That this race, dancing for their own pleasure in movement, have at once danced movements with purely theatrical lines is amazing. The Sevillanas was born so that the couple dancing might be amused and flirt with each other. Its primary scope is identical with that of the jitterbug. But the Sevillanas can be viewed from any angle, and the spectator will encounter a beauty of line and counter-line as perfect as the most perfect line planned by the greatest choreographer. It is possible that this unconscious creation of air design is due to the Iberian subconscious self-consciousness. He has a sixth sense which stands away and views him as others see him; and no less an artist than Eleonora Duse claimed that this sixth sense is what makes genius.

There is in the blood of the Spaniard such a choreographic unity that his every gesture is a "mauresque." A chulo, lighting his cigarette, moves his entire body down to his very feet, into a spiraled perfect balance to his lifted hands. It is a small ceremony and as such takes on rhythmic expression with an unforgettable change of mood and line. Otero writes that the children of Sevilla begin to dance as soon as they can move their little bodies. And the "abanecos de calena," those cheap fans sold at the Plaza de Toros, have printed on them gay coplas of the Sevillanas. The corrida itself is the most tragic and beautiful ballet that was ever staged: the torero creating consciously with his own slim glowing body and his plastic capa, balancing spiral lines to the unconscious curves of the charging black bull. It is this magnificent creation of beauty in counterline in the face of death that

[1] André Levinson, "Argentina," Editions des Chroniques du Jour, 1928, Paris.

the Spaniard cheers, not the danger and the death itself. ". . . and now there is one man, the matador, armed only with the cape and his skill and knowledge of bullfighting, meeting the bull alone, playing it, keeping it charging the cape and not himself, controlling the bull, steadying its rush, keeping it close to him, dominating it, holding it with the cloth as if it were a magnet, weaving the earth-shaking mass of savage flesh around his body as if it were something smooth and plastic, and doing all this, if he is doing it well, as smoothly and gently and gracefully as a dancer, sculpturing the poised and airy attitudes of his slender body against the dark, destroying mass of the bull, seemingly without effort, seemingly without risk. . . ." [2]

The Goyaesque beauty of Argentina lent itself perfectly to the interpretations of great Andalucian themes as classicized by Albeniz, Granados and De Falla. The sensuality was present without loss of pride or dignity. Tall and slim, Argentina lifted her arms in a wide brazeo which immediately became nearly a trademark of this new school. Her inspired, stirring romanticism was nowhere more perfectly demonstrated than in the "Cordoba" of Albeniz, and the second dance from De Falla's "Vida Breve." It is said that the art she created "was all her own" and was based on "her conviction that the dance must possess an inner content—communicate feeling—if it were to endure."

Most widely known for her control of the castanets, she was the first to make of these simple pieces of wood an instrument capable of evoking the whole gamut of the emotions. Heretofore, castanets had been exciting and joyous (a happy person is called "estar uno como unas castañuelas"). She made them sad and dramatic as well. With her long supple fingers she was able to control an instrument which was nearly man-size, and with these she introduced new rhythms and techniques to the repertoire.

She convinced the world that the Spanish dance possesses a technique which properly handled need not lean on any other school, but can stand alone, a classic structure as complete as the School of Ballet.

Otero spoke of Argentina with deepest respect, and said she was the soul of all that was noblest in Spain. She had worked hard for many years before the world gave her success. During her last tours she was ill and went through her performances only with the aid of medicaments. She died suddenly and easily after a happy day spent watching the Spanish folk dance, and a great glowing beauty went out of the world with her.

Hard on the heels of Argentina came Argentinita. Like her prede-

[2] Leslie Charteris, "Juan Belmonte," Doubleday, 1937, Garden City, New York.

ARGENTINITA

cessor of such a similar name, she had played the music halls and
cafetins of the world with tremendous success. Spain itself loved her
more than Argentina because she was "more Spanish." Her own contribution to the elevation of her country's art is tremendous. Had she
not appeared, the world might have thought that the Spanish dance-
style of Argentina was the result of an isolated genius. Argentinita
confirmed brilliantly the essential foundation of the renaissance
estilo. If, as some critics claim, she lacked the aspirational nobility
of line, the dramatic impact of objective emotionalism, which were
Argentina's, she entirely made up for that lack in her wit and earthy
understanding of her people. No artist has handled so flawlessly the
regional dance interpretation. The Sardana, the Charrada, the Bulerias, in her capable hands, became more than dances—they were a
psychological study of the folk. Her "bosquejos" (sketches) in themselves a definite contribution in a new concert form, are gems of
human and choreographic understanding.

Her death was a sharp and sudden blow to the dance world. She
might have lived a little longer if she had given up dancing—but that,
for her, would not have been living!

At the moment of this writing her beloved sister, Pilar Lopez of the
Maya-smile and the silver feet, is dancing in Madrid all the famous
repertoire of Argentinita. Perhaps she will take onto her slim shoulders the heavy mantle which has been laid down by Argentina and
Argentinita—the heart-breaking destiny of queen and pioneer of the
Spanish dance. Or those amazing young artists, Rosario and Antonio,
"Los Chavalillos Sevillanos" (The Kids from Sevilla), who since their
success in the Americas, have broadened their repertoire of Flamenco
and Andalucian themes to include the whole gamut of Iberian choreography, will heed the wide and enthusiastic public which hails them
as worthy successors to the crown of the Spanish dance.

Pure Spanish choreography is rapidly finding its way into the
repertoire of the ballet. For many years the Paris Opera retained Juan
Martinez to stage only Iberian works. His dances for "L'Illustre
Fragonard," with Laura St. Elmo dancing, were outstanding.

In this country the first step toward the recognition of renaissance
Spanish technique was the "Goyescas" choreographed by Fernandez.

"El Amor Brujo" by De Falla has been luckier than "El Sombrero
de Tres Picos" by the same composer. Written for Pastora Imperio—
("we believe in God when we look at Pastora"[3]) on a story told to
Martinez Sierra by Imperio's mother, this ballet is thoroughly gitano.
In 1915 Imperio danced it in Madrid. In 1928 Argentina produced it

[3] Carl van Vechten, "The Music of Spain" (quote of Benavente), Alfred A.
Knopf, 1918, New York.

Photo by Diaz and Rogers

ANTONIO and ROSARIO, "LOS CHAVALILLOS SEVILLANOS"

in Paris; and, in 1945, Argentinita's interpretation was in the repertoire of the Ballet Theater. Seldom touched by estranjero choreographers; and, among Iberians, danced only by Spain's greatest, the
stirring, earthy music in 1930 had yet to be interpreted to its composer's satisfaction.

"The Three-Cornered Hat" is better known generally as it has
been used more often in the ballet repertoire. But the choreography
of Massine, however brilliant is not of the Spanish school and has no
place in this book. Argentinita danced the miller's wife opposite Massine in 1943. Coming to my studio after rehearsing it, she was tired
and flushed. At the Metropolitan, startled by an unexpected and un-
Spanish lift to Massine's shoulder she had made short work of sub-
sequent choreographic sequences.

"And now, Madame," said Massine, "we two make a grand jeté en
tour across the stage." Argentinita lifted her brows. "No, Leonide,
you make it. I stand right here and play palillos."

It is our misfortune that the necessity for "great sums of money"
which prevented Argentina from bringing a company to the United
States, has also kept in Europe the presentation of other great all-
Spanish ballets. In 1927 Argentina staged Duran's ballet "El Fandango," and in 1928 Halffler's "Sonatina." Argentinita presented
Pittaluga's "La Romeria de los Cormidor" in 1933; and, in 1934 "Corrida de Fiesta" by the same composer. Argentina's last ballet production was in Paris in 1934, "El Contrabandista" by Espla.

Very recently in a conversation with Antonio (of Antonio &
Rosario) about the renaissance of the Spanish dance, the conclusion
was reached that the more recent major developments in the Spanish
dance have originated outside of Spain; such as the concert dance
finding its first audiences in Paris, and the Spanish ballet evolving in
New York. The Spanish dancer, staying at home, seems to be content
to perform the school and cafetin dances of fifty or a hundred years
ago. But the Spaniard, traveling abroad while remaining utterly Spanish, carrying his nationality about him like a mantle, yet is stimulated
by foreign art movements and so contributes to the flowering of his
own characteristic art (Argentina, Escudero, Argentinita, Martinez,
Antonio & Rosario and many others).

The realization that this renaissance has taken place within two
decades seems fantastic. There is no reason why this dance style shall
not in the very near future grow to be as established in public favor
as the ballet, which has reigned in the west for several centuries. The
Spanish dance is better equipped to take such a place than any other
dance-art. With the adoption of a universal system of teaching and a
widely understood terminology, it will be possible for the Spanish

JUAN MARTINEZ

choreographer to put out a call and gather together any number of dancers equipped to go into rehearsal and turn out as many ballets in a season as the classic ballet does.

The "Andaluces delicias" with the "honey in their hips" were fascinating Rome when the rest of Europe was half-savage, there is no reason why their lovely flower should not today bear the fruit of a complete and many-sided choreographic art.

Chapter

IX

T E C H N I Q U E

*T*he physical technique of any type of dancing is divided into four different groups. First, and most important is the carriage of the body. To the layman it may seem the least important as it is the least obvious, yet any dancer knows that an otherwise flawless technique can be spoiled by a poor carriage of the torso. Especially for the synthetic Spaniard is body-carriage important, for the essence of all characterization lies in the spinal column. Since body-carriage is generally considered God's gift to the genius it is rarely studied, and never with the proper intensity.

Nothing could be further from the perfect Spanish dancer's body than the body of the chic woman of today. Compare sketches in the fashion magazines with the round figure of Argentinita! The modish woman thrusts abdomen, shoulders, and head forward; her breasts fall, and she is without chest or hips; her backbone protrudes, curved as a bow, from her décolleté, and her hips and collar bones are without shame. The Spanish body is in direct contrast and thoroughly erect. Shoulders, abdomen and head are back, the chest is up, and breasts and hips are fulsome curves. The backbone curves inward at the waistline so that the entire line of the vertebrae is marked by an indent rather than chiropractic lumps. Below and between the shoulder-blades the back arches upward.

There is a flowing ease in this proud carriage that is found nowhere but in Spain. It is the common property of both male and female dancer who, in movement, seem so utterly different. "Of the existing national dance cults there is none which insists on such a rigid dis-

Photo by Marcus Blechman

WHITE MANTILLA—LILLIAN

Photo by Charles Clayton, Jr.

MANDROÑIO MANTILLA—CAROLA GOYA

tinction between the two sexes as that which for centuries has flourished in Spain." [1] The male dancer is asentao from the armpits to
knees. He dominates the woman at all times by sheer strength of controlled virility. He is the most thoroughly masculine of all male
dancers.

The woman swings her hips a little as one who carries something
heavy on her head. She has a veiled provocation in her walk. But the
foreigner must be very careful lest she exaggerate this and become
cheaply vulgar. This is the greatest pitfall of the foreigner; to give
vulgarity instead of sensuality. Exaggeration is never artistic. It must
be remembered that the essence of the Spanish dance is hard-held passion which, like water bubbling in a tea-kettle only now and then
pushes the lid up a little to boil over. There is a certain contraction
in all the muscles, and an almost oriental coldness of face, as though
the dancer knows that if he gives his temperament full rein its fire
would, like the Phoenix, verily consume him. Lacking the Spaniard's
natural sensuality, the foreigner attempts to compensate with dash
and coquetry in the popular dance and with vulgarity in the Flamenco. This way lies ruin. Neither is it necessary that you become
lost in sensuality at the moment of dancing. No great actor ever loses
himself so completely in his role that he forgets to stand mentally
away from himself and criticize his own effects. Study your movements until they "hold the mirror up to nature" and become the
replica of restrained passion. Naturally the restraint is in ratio to the
passion.

There is no part of the Spanish body in motion that is not balanced by the rest. This is an oriental heritage and is as natural as
breathing. Have you seen a Spanish woman with a fan? Not one who
is using that simple instrument to telegraph a hundred messages to an
admirer. No, just any fat dueña buying safety-pins in a tiny, hot
store. The unceasing opening and closing of the fan, the rapid little
wavings and pointings and gesturings and goodness knows what else!
It is a third hand, that fan, and it is never at any moment other than
a fluttering bird of grace, while head, eyes and hands follow to balance its rapid movements. This living of rhythmic movement is
strictly Spanish, and springs from a subconscious consciousness of the
watcher. It is a rich inheritance of blood and of environment. But the
Anglo-Saxon has conquered by stubborn study many things. If he sees
beauty; if he desires it; and if he works seriously and patiently then
that fascinating smoothness of body co-ordination may be his.

To begin with; pull the shoulders back and down until the shoulder-

[1] Cyril Rice, "Escudero," Souvenir Program.

Photo by Boris Bakchy

PILAR GOMEZ and ROZZINO

blades are flat, and keep them there through any and all convolutions
of the arms and waist. The chest is up and out always, as though a cord
from between the breasts suspended the body from the ceiling. The
Spanish woman is proud of her breasts. Often she drapes her manton
in such a way that only their swelling fullness keeps the shawl around
her shoulders. If the chest and shoulders assume the proper position,
the hips will fall back into the proper position more easily. Take care
that the abdomen is held in, and that the waist is cambré. Bring
back the head until there is a plumb line from the base of the skull to
the back between the shoulders; tilt up the chin. "Lift the upper body
toward the ceiling and drive the lower body into the floor" says
Beaucaire-Montalvo, veteran teacher. This position must be assumed
and practiced at all times—walking on the street, at parties, in class,
everywhere, until the stiffness disappears and it becomes a natural carriage to the aspirant.

There is little or no actual change of bodily carriage during the
dance. The famous "back-bend" [2] is in the spine *above* the waist and is
often far more of a side-bend than it appears. I cannot over-emphasize
the importance of carriage. In the down-held shoulder, the cambré
back, and up-held upper-arm lie the strongest physical characterization
of Spanish dancing. Do not exaggerate! Pulse to the music! Do not be
afraid to be still! Do not be ashamed to be sex-conscious!

Second of the four types of physical movement in the dance is that
of the arms and shoulders. In Spain they have, at all times, a characteristic contra-line. I have said that the shoulders are always back and
down (the forward upward shrug being employed only for special
expression and then irrespective of the movement of the arms). Care
must be taken to keep them thus, or the entire line of the arm will be
lost. From this down-held shoulder the elbow is turned out, up
and well away from the rib-cage. Lift the arms to leave the body
"draughty." The attention is on the *upper* arms, which Delsarte says,
is the sensual part. If shoulder and elbow are held properly, the forearm when relaxed will find its proper position with the arms in the
first, the second, and the sixth position. This same line is approxi-
mately the same when the arms are in the other positions. Care must
be taken not to lift the shoulders when the arms are in fifth, while the
forearm still curves forward in this position.

In the Andalucian dance the arm movements flow subtly into each
other scarcely ever stopping in a given position. In the Flamenco
dance the hands and wrists take on an amazing and difficult sinuosity.

Working from first position and keeping the shoulder and upper

[2] Perfectly exemplified in Pilar Gomez.

arm immobile, turn the back of the hand toward the body, fingers easily straightened and slightly apart. Describing a quarter-circle with the hand, rotate the wrist until the fingers point toward the floor. Continue circle until the palm of the hand is toward the body, then the fingers close into the palm. In this semi-fist, the wrist is turned up and around into the original position while the fingers are opened to recommence the movement. This sinuous twisting of the wrist is used in all positions and is alternated in the Flamenco dances with palmadas and pito.

Always take great care to control the arms. Never fling them about, and do not use castañuelas until you are able to do so without any constriction in the arm movements. Never let the elbow drop. Never lift the shoulders without *willing* an effect. Study the arm movements so that the head and torso follow characteristically. The arms indicate a curved air design—part of a moving body which is the heart of the prized Moorish design of the capital letter "S."

The brazeo, or carriage of the arms is, in the first five positions, virtually the same as the five positions of the ballet. As a practical aid two more positions are added:

      1st —Chest high, fingers nearly touching in front
      2nd—Shoulder-high, and extended at the sides
      3rd —One arm above the head, the other in 2nd
      4th —One arm above head, the other in 1st
      5th —Both arms above head, fingers nearly touching
      6th —Extended 5th, arms lifted in "Y"
      7th —Arms at waist, either behind or at sides.

Third of the four types of physical movement is that of the lower limbs. The difference in the carriage of the legs, knees, and feet, between the Spaniard and the Anglo-Saxon is so subtle as to be felt rather than seen by the uninitiated. Both in clothing and movement, legs must be modestly unobtrusive. Almost never is the foreleg lifted higher than parallel with the floor, rare exceptions being in the province of the virtuose of Iberian blood, and better excluded entirely from the foreigner's repertoire of steps. A Spaniard can do *anything*, and it is Spanish. The foreigner may do only that which is done by the *majority* of Spaniards and has therefore become Spanish in itself.

The legs, like the arms are controlled. Movements all curve inward and are seldom large in the Anglo-Saxon sense of proportion, being never *thrown* beyond the muscular possibility of control (as is, for example, the high-kick). As the average Spanish physique is compact, it follows that height cannot come into the province of that physique's

Six Photos by Mario Rosel

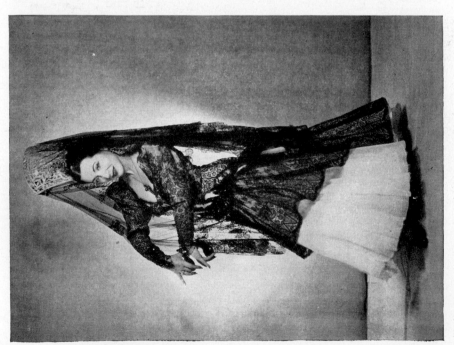

a. First position

BRAZEO—LA MERI

b. Second position

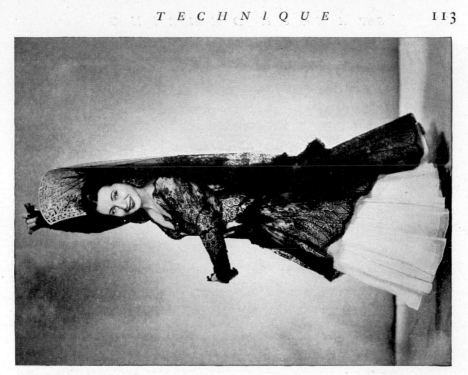

d. Fourth position

c. Third position

f. Seventh position

BRAZEO—LA MERI

e. Fifth position

control. Possibly for this reason, rotation of the hip-joint is seldom
if ever used. But rotation in the knee-joint is very characteristic. This
rotation is never terminated in a sharp snap, tautness in the knees and
ankles not being of the Spanish school. Much can be obtained by the
foreigner if, in the early weeks of his study, he practices relaxation
in the knees whenever the leg is in the air. It seems paradoxical to
advise this when I have so recently spoken of the control of the Spanish dancer. Yet it must be remembered that there is Moorish blood
in the southern dance, and the Oriental ever finds little for his feet
to do save mark the rhythm, while his arms and upper-body do the
dancing. By contrast the occidental does all his dancing with his legs.
So for the Anglo-Saxon the difficulty is to learn a certain tautness of
the arms and body and to *forget* a certain tautness of the legs. The
Spanish dance is "the eternal battlefield" with "the blood of the van-
quished feverishly battling in the arteries of the vanquisher." [3]

Otero made use of the ballet positions of both arms and feet after
his return from Stockholm. However, it is understood that the feet
are by no means turned out at the ninety-degree angle of the ballet.
In the Andalucian dance they are at forty-five degrees; in the
Flamenco, straight forward.

    1st —heels together
    2nd—heels some six inches apart, weight evenly distributed
    3rd —one heel against the other arch
    4th —one foot before the other (*planta natural*)
    5th —front heel to back toe.

Ellis has said that the Spaniards are fascinated by sound. Surely the
Flamenco dance is largely based on the syncopated, rhythmic and
contrapuntal sound of staccato heels and toes. The variety of these
is limited only by the technical skill of the performer, and aside from
a few brief notes on style, the field is entirely open to the invention
of the dancer.

First of all the toes must be pointed forward, not outward. Second,
the knees must be bent as little as possible. Cyril Rice has written that
when Escudero does taconeo, "his legs ripple." This is the effect of
a fast taconeo with a nearly unbent knee.

The sound must be sharp and clean, the *pica* or stroke with the
ball of the foot being as clear and as loud as the *taco* (heel).

These rules are in power whether the dance be Flamenco, agitanado,
or classic.

[3] André Levinson, "Argentina," Editions des Chroniques du Jour, 1928,
Paris.

Below are some preliminary exercises for taconeo. ("Toe" means the ball of the foot; the *pica*. "Heel" means the heel, or *taco*. "Stamp" means the whole sole.)

| Left-
toe-heel | Right
toe-heel | (To be done en place) |

| Left
Stamp | Right
toe-heel | Left
toe-heel | (To be done alternating, the stamp
forward, the toe-heel en place) |

(The above step may also be done by facing right, with the right toe pointed outward when the right stamp is done. The same on the left.)

| Left
heel-stamp
and   1 | Right
heel-stamp
and   2 | (To be done en place and traveling for-
ward) |

| Right
toe-heel | Left
heel-stamp | (This is the *redoble*. Preceded and fol-
lowed by a stamp becomes a *des-
plante*) |

Never overreach. The feet almost invariably play close about each other, and the floor design is small. Never spread the knees. Spanish knees almost cling to each other. Never fling the legs. Keep the thighs together. Never try to astonish by acrobacy; by heighth of développé nor depth of back-bend. The dance is rhythmic not acrobatic. Relax. Take it easy. Don't fling! Cling! Spaniards do not work at their dancing. They *love* it into life.

Last and most important of the quartette of physical techniques of the dance is that of facial expression. It is subtle and personal and difficult to teach. Mirror of the soul, it must be dominated from within, and the teacher can do little save indicate the general lines of thought by which may be reached the state of mind which produces the delicate, fleeting exteriorization of the soul of the Spanish dance. An understanding of the spiritual background will, doubtless, not only quite spontaneously take care of the facial expression, but will draw together and give to the whole that inner ecstasy of true art.

All these techniques are natural to the Spaniard, and so the Spanish maestro could and did teach through dances. But without the blessing of Iberian blood, the student must *first* make these techniques a part of himself. Spiritual moralizing is a means of personal evaluation in study and must not be synthetically applied. A mirror will not teach you the Spanish dance.

Is there one who knows Andalucia who does not know that pride is her chief characteristic? In the dancer this pride is overweening until it nearly reaches scorn. It is an expression of face and eyes and head which silently says "Here am I!" The control of felt excitement in the dancer is the result of this proud dignity.

In the patio the Andalucian dances for his partner, on the café stage for his audience. The facial expression is guarded, restrained, but there is a certain veiled challenge, a discreetly-expressed assurance of approval. The man wears an aloof dignity, the woman a proud coquetry. Eyes are endlessly expressive, the habitual scowl of the brows belied by the soft light of the eye itself, and the slight and sudden tilt of the head. On an instant a flashing smile breaks through, only to be lost again under an expression of indifference.

The flamenco dances for himself. One cannot guess what thoughts go on behind his impassive face and half-closed eyes; but one feels a very electric current of seething, passionate joy in the atmosphere which surrounds him. His mouth almost never breaks its immobility, but when he lifts his eyes they express the whole gamut of the emotions.

To give rules for expression is impossible. We can notate the positions of the arms and legs, but only the Hindu can do as much for the brows and eyes. For anyone with a healthy body can learn to dance but the quintessence of expression is the prerogative of the true artist, and he must find it in himself. I can only say not to be afraid to study every changing expression; to strive to be a hard critic of yourself; and, to forever seek to love and understand the passionate, hermetic soul of Andalucia. Technique is a means to an end, not an end in itself. It is only the vehicle of your expression. It must be learned to be forgotten. Or, rather, it must be remembered by the muscles and forgotten by the mind .

Carmen de Toledo, "gitana pura," teaches through jaleo. She drives home even the fundamental steps by a series of gritos, taconeo, and palmadas. A bundle of energy, she takes pupil after pupil in half-hour private sessions all day long, and each lesson is punctuated by her own wild taconeo and heart-raising shouts. She believes that the *soul* must be learned at once with the step, so that the two will nevermore be separated from each other.

Never fix a smile and leave it there.
Never be hard in any expression.
Never overreach nor overwork.
And in all things—face, body, arms and legs—never exaggerate.

Sombrero Cordovez—Carmen de Toledo

Photo by Philcox

FELUCCA—JUANA

Photo by Marcus Blechman

SOMBRERO DE QUESO—LILIAN

MANOLO VARGAS

There is a very definite difference between the masculine and feminine style of dancing flamenco. The man takes great pride in his
strength and virility. No line or gracia is allowed to enter which
might be construed as "merengue" (sweet). His body is asentao;
his air design, sharp angles; his phrasing, abrupt. Often-quoted is the
statement of Vincente Escudero, "If only one person said my dancing
was effeminate, I would never dance again!" His dancing is "willful,
savage, serious and fantastic." Some gitanos despise even the use of
castanets as smacking of effeminacy, and use a resounding *pito* of
three of four fingers in each hand. Escudero even created "ritmos"
(rhythms) with his finger-nails. Manolo Vargas, lithe gitano, learned
castanets (together with regional dance) only when he joined Argentinita's ensemble.

By contrast the dancing of the gitana is all that is feminine. Her
air design is curves and convolutions; the "mauresque," the spiral in
which all lines of motion return to the center force. Sallilas says this
center force is the base of the backbone, which in the Andalucian
woman is actually more curved than in any other race; Carreras says
this center force is in the pelvis. In costume as in movement the gypsy
woman accentuates the mystery of the body, indicating subtly the
seduction of hidden beauty. Paul Reboux writes, "This Flamenco
dance represents all passion in three acts; desire, seduction, conclusion.
It is at once a comedy and a drama. They say that it takes fifteen
years to form a flamenca dancer, for she should be fifteen to mime
the first part, twenty to mime the second, and thirty to mime the
third." [4] Writes Arthur Symons, "The gypsy coiled about the floor,
in her trailing dress never so much as showing her ankles with a
rapidity concentrated upon itself; her hands beckoned, reached out,
clutched delicately, lived to their finger-tips. . . . Then the movement
became again more vivid, more restrained as if teased by some unseen
limits, as if turning upon itself in vain desire of escape; more feverish,
more fatal, the humor turning painful with the pain of achieved desire; more eager with the langour in which desire dies triumphant." [5]

To the gypsy the dance is a prayer to all desire, all consummation.
It is the expression of the elemental truth that all life is birth and
mating and death. It is the teasing wit, the gaminerie of the first
flirtatious look, or the fatal impact of a sudden overwhelming desire;
it is the challenge and the pursuit, the voluptuous game of love and
desire. The hard pressed climb of the vertiginous slope of mounting

[4] Paul Reboux, "Teresina," Souvenir Program, 1932.
[5] Arthur Symons, quoted from Carl van Vechten's "Music of Spain," Alfred
A. Knopf, 1918, New York.

Photo by Boris Bakchy

CARMEN AMAYA and HER SISTERS

passion and the headlong plunge to the destruction when one seems "the master of all the kingdoms of the world." [6]

All the body takes part in the dance. Cervantes writes that the gypsy Preciosa "prayed with her feet"; but, the limitation is poetic license, for being gypsy, she danced not only with tapping feet, but with knees which bend and sway under the surge of passion; with the "admirable haunches" that so enchanted Chabrier; with the bending, twisting waist, built by nature itself, to express her voluptuous imagination; with her curving shoulders and her undulating seeking arms and slender, promising finger-tips begging for sanctuary; with her head, and her eyes, and her flashing teeth, and her very heart. And at the end she throws her handkerchief into the lap of a chosen admirer as do her sisters in the cafés of North Africa.

"The dance is not a spectacle for the amusement of a languid and passive public as with us. It is rather the visible embodiment of an emotion in which every spectator takes an active and helpful part." [7] So the aim is to excite, not to astonish. The circle into which the dancer steps is a choreographic unity with her. At the very beginning she asks their help.... "Darme ustes argunas parmitas seccas para ver si vengo en conocimiento." ... The palmadas are hers as she begins; someone beats a "style-stick" on a chair-rung; another sits forward and begins a building contra-tempo with his heels; "Olé" they encourage at first. And then as the dance progresses, as the juerga grows warmer and more excited, the cries are sharper, the palmadas and contra-zapateo louder; Anda! Anda! Salero, Chica! Que gracia! Agua, agua!

Says Argentinita, "The gypsies are the truest artists I know. They dance not for money or applause, but for their own pleasure and satisfaction." "He sings and dances to relieve his feelings." [8] They have their own code and their own ways. They are passionate and jealous and hermetic; they are thieves and cheats and great artists.

Since man could write it seems professional pen-sters have applied their talent and fire to descriptions of the Flamenco dance. Yet, when all has been said ... what has been said? If you have not seen it yourself and seen it with your heart as well as with your eyes, none of this poesy brings to the imagination anything like an adequate description. If you have seen it yourself, all this poesy is beggared by the thing itself. Why is this? The dance is not so beautiful? Lovelier women have moved more beautiful bodies with more grace. It is not

[6] Ibn el Fared—Arab poet—1220 A. D.
[7] Havelock Ellis, "Soul of Spain," Houghton Mifflin Co., 1909, Boston.
[8] Gilbert Chase, "Music of Spain," W. W. Norton & Co., Inc., 1941, New York.

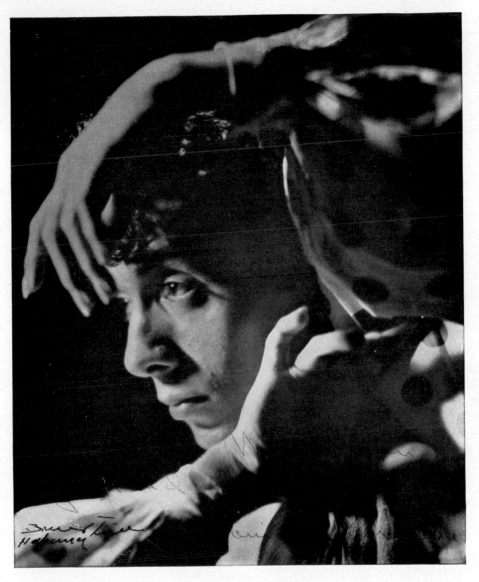

ANTONIO DE CORDOBA

unique in its emotional fire. There is fire in Scotland and in Russia. Perhaps it is because the Flamenco dance is not a part of life but is life itself. The dancing "roms" to whom all life finds expression in song and dance, set among the Andalucians who were themselves "born to dance," have created an expression so rich in sincerity that it touches even the most cynical. It is this very sincerity which grips and stirs beyond all description. And it is in this sincerity that the "ersatz" flamenco fails. We can and do learn the technique which is, after all, limited. We are honest, we are objective, we are artistic . . . but are we sincere? Do we move because we want to be seen moving, or because we *must* move to express an inexpressible racial sorrow? I am endlessly interested in this elusiveness of the Flamenco spirit. What is the "lowest common denominator"? For if I can reduce it to that, I can solve it all. Or must each find the answer secretly within himself? I don't believe it! The very gypsies themselves tell and discuss endlessly their feelings, their tragedies, their psychological problems. Typically enough the conclusions which I have reached in my years of teaching are negative ones. You can't force it, and you can't hurry it, and you can't fake it, and you can't steal it. It must come to you in its own good time; it must be completely honest, and it must be completely yours. Like the proverbial hare the jerky "inamorata" sprints wildly, but sleeps through the crucial moments of unfolding. Fifteen years ago I danced Farruca and Bulerias with the gitanas and was taken for one of them. But today there are times when the alegrias still eludes me and I have grown to heartily dislike the cursed thing. Yet who knows, one day when I have completely turned away from it, perhaps it will come to me.

Argentinita, finest protagonist of the Flamenco dance on the concert stage and herself pure Castilian, says that for many years she feared to join the dancing groups of gypsies, but it was not until she lost this fear and forced herself to join in the Bulerias that she considered herself a true Spanish dancer.

It is said that Otero himself could and did dance a cañi as any Cale, but that he never succeeded in imparting it to any of his pupils.

Technique we can teach, but experience must be bought—the hard way—and the Flamenco dance is the product of emotional experience; and, in its finest perfection must be imbued with that matchless pride which is the heritage of the Sudras.

Chapter

X

C A S T A N E T S

astanets are, perhaps, the most characteristic accessory of the Spanish dance. Andalucians call them "palillos"; Valencians call them "postizos"; Aragonesas call them "pulgaretes"; Castilians call them "castañuelas"; and, foreigners call them "castanets." Doña Paulina, great old teacher of Barcelona, said there is no such word as "castanets," that they are a purely Spanish instrument and so there is no reason for naming them in anything but Spanish.

The exact origin of castanets is lost in the mists of antiquity. We know that the gaditanes used them when they conquered fashionable Rome. We know that the Moors have used chinchines for many centuries. One of the stylized designs of ancient China is a pair of castanets, called "pans." Today in India, dancers use a long narrow pair of wooden clappers called "bhajinnas," or "chittakas," which are represented in Greek friezes. Instruments similar to these are seen in the hands of dancers in the Egyptian paintings. Also we have the description written 13 B.C. by a gentleman of Syracuse, at a banquet in Memphis, of a pair of Egyptian dancers who performed to the music they themselves made with small wooden clappers held in the hands. The priests of Hathor of Egypt were represented as "clattering castanets"; Herodotus describes Egyptian women as playing castanets and tambourines; and an irritated Arabian once replied to a broadcast of mine, that castanets like practically everything else, originated with the Arabs. The Spanish name "castañuelas" is supposed to be derived from the shape of the instrument which is similar to a castaña shell.

Photo by H. Golden

LA MAJA—CAROLA GOYA

Photo by Mario Rosel

LA MANOLA—LA MERI

Like violins, castanets can be bought at any price and of any tone. Again like violins, bad ones can be bought anywhere, while those of perfect tone are as rare as the Stradivarius. And there are many dancers who would refuse the price of that famous fiddle rather than part with their own beloved palillos. For the tone mellows and grows with age, gaining with the heat and oily dampness of the hand a quality of voice otherwise unattainable. Besides, those whose wood and whose carving have combined to produce perfection of tone are rare indeed. The key-tone of a pair of castanets will change from one pair of hands to another, and so are said to take on the personality of the artist.

Commercial castanets like commercial violins abound. Germany produced large ones of Andalucian line whose voice is hearteningly noisy, but whose tone gives no crescendo, and does not improve the usage. The United States has invented the rubberized instrument—the delight of the beginner—easy to handle, never breaks, is low-priced and has no character.

In Valencia they make postizos of a distinctly different cut from the Andalucian. They have a narrower and squarer neck. Most of the castanets acquired by tourists are this shape. A coat of varnish adds to their appearance and completely destroys the tone, and they are then only good for hanging on the wall.

In Sevilla one may, if one knows where to look, find excellent palillos at high, yet commercial prices. There is one man in the city who makes them, but he has hidden himself away and will see no one. The best of his produce went to José Otero, the teacher; the rest to a music shop in the Calle Sierpes (Antonio Damas). Among the palillos which came into Otero's expert hands, there were at times a pair which several years of care would make into an excellent solo instrument. But the perfect castañuelas, those of great age, of range of voice, of personality, in short, the "palillos Stradivarius," are or were, the property of the great artists and are now cherished as the rarest treasure by those who understand; or they are lying dusty and forgotten in the lost corner of a pawnshop. The perfect pair for *you* can only be found when you have trained yourself to know them when you see them.

Castanets range in size from 4 centimeters in diameter (even the babies dance in Spain!) to 7 centimeters, or men's size. They must be found to fit the hand. You will note that La Argentina used rather large ones because her fingers were long and supple, while Amalia Molina having small, round hands, used a much smaller size. They can be made of any exceptionally hard wood, grenadilla being most generally used. Ebony is sometimes employed, but is so brittle as to break very easily. The poetic little ivory ones of a decade past are dainty but voiceless. Espinillo and acacia can be used, but the best wood is grenadilla; the white markings which one often sees on castanets, is the white ring around the too-small heart of the tree. Effectively these markings do not hurt the tone, but, because of their rarity, an all-dark pair are considered superior. The key-tone is regulated by the depth and size of the "huevo" or "corazon" (hollow) and the accuracy of the "punto" or "beco" (the lower point where the shells actually strike). Ease of control is achieved by a master-maker of palillos, in the angle of the "orejas" (holes) and the curve of the "puente" (the place within the string-holes where the two shells touch).

The fascinating red and yellow ribbons which decorate the strings of commercial postizos should be dispensed with since they complicate playing. For certain period dances or special effects they may be added, but are never necessary.

The peasant often wears his pulgaretes on the middle finger. The undecorated dry "tak" thus produced is pleasing when used in groups and as accompaniment to dances of the soil. Also the gitanas of Sacro-Monte, in adopting palillos for the delectation of the tourist, have found the middle-finger technique more suitable to the resounding cueva. They manage an ingenious double-clop with the left hand, which produces an excellent effect when used, as they invariably do, in group dancing.

But the Andalucian, the virtuoso, attaches the palillos to his thumbs. The twelve-inch cord which passes through the orejas must be thick enough to amply fill these holes. The extreme ends of the cord are knotted, then the longer end is tied around the shorter to produce a slip-knot. The instruments are applied to the thumbs as in illustration, page 132, with the knot nearest the hand, taking care that the knot is directly on top of the thumb. The cord must be pulled tight enough to *force* the thumb-knuckle to a slight bend. As properly made castañuelas are voiced one a third above the other, the high (or tenor) goes on the right-hand; the low (or bass) on the left. When the respective voices are carefully determined, it is well to make a small mark on the tenor instrument to serve as identification in moments of haste.

The left hand marks the beat, while the right one makes the "carretillas" or "barrigas" (trills) and contratempes. To make the carretillas, flex the right thumb until the castanets stand a little apart, the lower one resting on the cushion of the thumb. Now let three fingers, beginning with the little finger, slip from the side of the top shell into the palm of the hand, while the index finger, striking immediately

Castanets by Carreras; Photo by Mario Rosel

a. "Ta"—posed by La Meri

Castanets by Carreras; Photo by Mario Rosel
b. Beginning of "Tara"—posed by La Meri

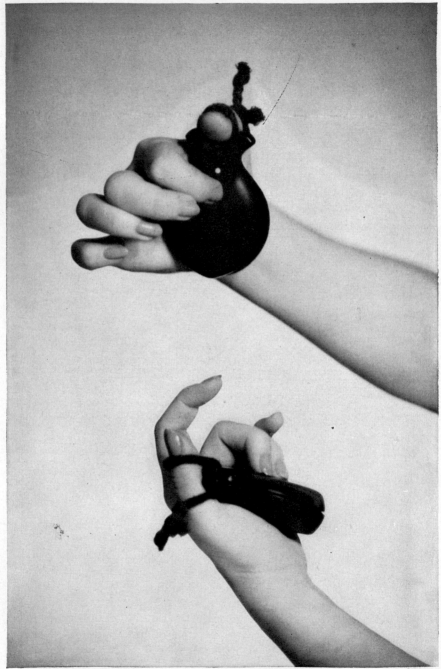

Castanets by Carreras; Photo by Mario Rosel

c. END OF "TARA"—posed by LA MERI

Castanets by Carreras; Photo by Mario Rosel

d. "Tok"—posed by La Meri

thereafter, lifts from the shell. Thus you obtain four evenly spaced blows, or "toks," which, when practice gives speed, becomes the carretilla. One should not wear long nails on the right hand. The single stroke of the bass is produced by striking the middle and ring fingers against the shell. The single stroke in the right hand is produced in the same way as the single stroke of the left. Suppleness in the wrists is difficult to obtain but necessary to perfect control.

The steady trill is done by repeated carretillas *evenly and rhythmically* spaced with the left stroke timing the music—one carretilla to each stroke of the left hand.

In beginning to learn to play castanets hold the arms curved to the front, the palms turned obliquely upward (page 133). As control is acquired the following exercise should be adopted. Stand weight on the right foot and facing left, left foot pointed front, arms above head in 5th position. Bring left arm out to 2nd, up in front of face and back to 5th to complete a circle. As left hand joins right in 5th, shift the weight to the left foot, face right, and repeat the exercise with the right arm.

The basic strokes given in the table may be varied according to the technical efficiency and contrapuntal knowledge of the performer.

To annotate the strokes of the castanets the following syllables are used:

Ta	Single stroke, left hand
Ti	Single stroke, right hand
Tara	Carretillas
Tok	Single stroke, both hands.

The numbers in the table denote the counts in the musical measure:

Waltz	1	2	and	3							
	Tok	Ta	Tara	Ta							

Pasodoble	1	2	and	3	4						
	Tok	Ta	Tara	Ta	Tok						

Jota	1	and	2	and	3	and					
	Ta	Ti	Ta	Ti	Ta	Ti					

Sevillanas	1	and	2	and	3	and	4	and	5	and	6	and
	Ta	Tara	Ta	Tara	Ta	Ti	Ta	Tara	Ta	Tara	Ta	Ti

Chapter

X

EXPERIENCES IN SPAIN

Since finishing this book it has been suggested to me that the reader would be interested in hearing some of the background which colors the study of the Spanish dance. There was quite some time that the student was unable to go into Spain; and, it seems like it will be another fairish time before crossing to Europe will be entirely easy. I, myself, had for years looked forward to the close of the Spanish Civil War, with the desire to return. Plans were made to go from Buenos Aires in the fall of 1939. But war was declared in Europe, and my contracts were "blacked out"—the trip to Spain was put off for a happier moment.

My own beginnings as a Spanish dancer seem to me amazingly unsensational. That generations of the proper chemical mixture of various nationalities should have produced just me, rather recalls the labor of the mountain. Still and all, there it is. I would surely never have been an interpreter of racial dances with an insatiable interest in folk arts and crafts, if certain persons back in Europe had not married each other. I am part Scot, who is no mean dancer himself, and whose music with its drone accompaniment and infinite tone-shadings recalled the Eastern music and the Cante Jondo (deep song gitano). I am part French, and the Frenchman has been a patron of the dance since France was France. I am part Welsh, and everyone knows the Welsh are like the Galicians, and great artists. And I am part Spanish, "and never was Spanish woman born who was not born to dance." [1]

[1] Saavedra de Cervantes, 1547-1616.

There were never professional artists in our family before, but every mother's son of them were great amateurs. On my father's side, the brothers made a stringed orchestra in their own family, and my grandmother living in a period when ladies didn't go on the stage, had a small theater built into her home. Of course, they were all Americans by then, having helped in the making of that flag with the thirteen stars.

I was born in Kentucky, which is a very nice place—but doesn't have the right atmosphere for budding tonadilleras; so destiny took a hand and moved us south to Texas. Down on the Mexican border, living took on something of the tempe of Latinism. I studied ballet; I learned the Mexican dances. And one day at a Mexican variety theater I saw a young girl who was a great Spanish dancer. It was La Argentina, though the name meant nothing to me then. It is hard to remember what I felt; what determination formed in me; whether or not I saw a clear goal. I know I found somewhere a bad pair of castañuelas, and I went home and taught myself to play them—wrong, of course! I saw Ruth St. Denis that year, too, and I knew that *just* Spanish dancing wouldn't be enough, sensing even then the kinship between Iberia and the East. But that is part of another story. I taught myself Spanish dancing, for there were no teachers of it down there. I haunted the Mexican theater and became one of the most accomplished dance-thieves you ever saw—stealing steps and lines and ideas from the first row in the balcony. Then mother and I went to Spain! We couldn't stay long because we didn't have much money. But we looked on the beauty of Madrid and of Sevilla, and then we went to Barcelona and I studied with Doña Paulina.

Doña Paulina is probably dead now. She was well past seventy when I knew her in 1922. She held her classes in a dingy room over the Lyric Theater, and most of her pupils were from the State Ballet Corps. She herself was a shapeless, fat mass in a colorless "mother hubbard." Her wisps of gray hair were squeezed into an infinitesimal chignon. She had only two or three yellow teeth, and her feet were thrust into heelless carpet-slippers. She sat down most of the time, teaching by shouting witticisms at her perspiring pupils. But if ever she heaved her waistless bulk from the chair and took the floor for a few steps, she showed to her blooming young students the meaning of artistry. She was the embodiment of "salero" (pep) and femininity. It is hard to believe, but it is true. Age had not dimmed the luster of her great black eyes and she knew how to express everything with them, with her castañuelas, and with the tilt of her head and shoulders.

I learned the Jota first and so sore did it make me that I could

LA MERI's unsensational beginning at the age of twelve

scarcely clamber up the stairways. There were no loafers with Doña Paulina. We used to sit in a circle for castañuela practice and one by one Doña would signal us to stop. Heaven help the last one, which was usually the worst (me!) left plonking pathetically alone!

I went home to Texas from Spain and got a job in the local theater doing "prologues" to the movies. I thought then that it was good because it was lucrative and fun. I know now that it was good because it taught me a great deal about stagecraft. There is no mistake so complete as trying to step from the studio onto the concert stage, for it is very necessary to serve an apprenticeship in cabaret, in vaudeville, or in musical comedy. After a winter of local professionalism, what more inevitable than that I should go to New York. I had no connections, no introductions, and very little sense. I took the classified Telephone Directory and started out to contact all the theatrical agents listed. There were hayseeds hanging out of my ears, and I turned down good jobs and accepted bad ones just because I didn't know any better. I had a week here, a week there; the movie houses; the subway circuit. But I was learning something about the show business and something about myself. Someway I got connected with Maria Montero, and seeing her cleared up the darkness of doubt. I knew what I had to.do, and I did it. I danced in her group for nothing on the agreement that I could steal everything from her I could get. She was a great dancer and a.deeply generous soul. God rest her. She was shot to death by a jealous lover at the foot of the altar in her home. She was buried in the manton given her by King Alphonso XIII of Spain—she, with her Bourbon face! Dramatic end for a Spanish dancer.

Presently Maria dissolved her group, and I was out of a job again, but much better equipped to keep the next one I got. I gave an audition for an agent, a charming gentleman. He liked my work, but confessed he understood nothing of "real" Spanish dancing. He phoned a colleague in the concert field who was a Spaniard. This Spaniard came over. I danced "Miranda a España" (Maria's routine). The Spaniard didn't say much, but I reckon he saw something there. "Where have you danced?" he asked. I had learned that on Broadway one must never, never admit that one has had no experience. I also knew that my prologue work at home stamped me as a small-town celebrity (Broadway's abomination). So I'd made up my safe little lie, and now I recited it. "In Mexico City." So few Americans had been there. *I* never had. "What theater?" "Teatro Nacional." The Spaniard smiled. "That is very strange. It isn't yet finished." But he took an exclusivity contract and presently got me an engagement in Mexico City. How beautiful that city is! I danced in the St. Regis

MARIA MONTERO

Dinner Club and afterwards at the Auto Show in the National Theater. My debut at the St. Regis was very swell, and starred with social and political celebrities. I entered in a white "mantilla" (lace head-scarf) and a white lace Spanish costume with a cascade of natural flowers adorning it. I did my paseo di gracia to polite applause. I made a quick turn to begin "Miranda a España." Then both feet went up and I sat down with such a thud that natives suspected an earthquake. My "peineta" (comb) dropped over one eye, and I broke off a heel and ruined my castañuelas. And all I could do was sit and laugh. But then the applause was very real, and when I came back after changing shoes and castañuelas, my success was assured.

I had a beautiful month there! I danced in the bullring at a monster benefit with the great Orquestra Tipica, partnered by a famous Mexican who taught Pavlowa the Jarabe. I saw all the Spanish artists who came there, good and bad, and from each I learned something. I attended corridas where the best of Mexican and Spanish toreros appeared.

I studied "capa" (cape) work with a bullfighter. He taught me many of the more beautiful figures. I even learned to do some of them creditably while being charged by a bicycle with bull horns on the handle-bars; which is the trick used for training the novices nowadays. It is a fascinating study and one I would heartily recommend to baritones planning to sing "Carmen"! I have worked at it at various times in my career—in Spain, in Mexico, in Peru—wherever I found a torero with fine style. The technique changes a little with the years. I know my last lesson differed in style from my first. And de Toledo, who studied with Gaona, has a very different and more formal and florid style.

One day in Lima as I sat eating luncheon, a gentleman approached our table. He was not tall, and he was not handsome, for he had the face of a gitano. But he carried himself like a prince, or a dancer, or a bullfighter, and the whole room turned to admire him. Arriving beside us, he bowed and asked pardon for his temerity, but last night he had seen me dance "La Corrida" and he could not but permit himself the honor to say "so one danced the bullfight." And he bowed and went away. But I cannot tell you the lift of his head, the pride in his eye. I could have thrown my sombrero to him in that moment for his very salero, even as he was throwing his to me!

Back in New York, I starred in a "flash act" for Keith Time called "Sevilla." Here a Shubert scout found me and booked me for the "Night in Spain." And soon afterwards it was decided that I had served my apprenticeship, and I got down to the real work of my life—concert.

LA MERI at the Don Quixote Fountain in Mexico City

This is the story of learning Spanish dancing, not the story of my life, so I won't tell you about my long tour in South America, which is itself so redolent of Spain in every way. How I haunted the theaters where Iberian artists played; how I took lessons from any who had time to teach me; how beautifully I was received (and taken for Spanish) by the Spanish colonies everywhere.

After South America I went back to Spain! This time just to Andalucia. What can I not say of Sevilla the beautiful? The Guadalquivir slipping by like a ribbon of silver; the Alcazar leaping toward the sky; the Cruz de Mayo in its delicate square.

Friends who write from Sevilla say it hasn't changed much during the war; that the Andalucian still "waits for the corrida and contemplates the zapateado." I hope with all my heart they are right. I remember walking to Otero's studio through the narrow cobbled streets. Whitewashed houses shouldered the street, and since there was seldom a sidewalk, one scrooged against their chalky walls to allow the old victoria carriages to pass. Each house had its wrought-iron gate, and behind it lay the blue-tiled, be-flowered patios around which the home was built. I became a confirmed "patio-peeker," peering into those Moorish interiors to enjoy vicariously the pleasure of the maid watering the flowers or the Señora ordering her house. And in how many houses one could hear the clop-clop of castañuelas, or a voice raised in Cante Jondo!

Otero's studio. A whitewashed house like all the others with a wrought-iron gate. Being a bachelor-establishment there were few flowers in the cool patio. To the right was the dancing-room. About twenty feet square, this room is historic. The walls are covered with colored posters of the bullfight; the floor, filthy with three generations of taconeo, sags and bounces when danced upon. Chaste wooden benches line the walls, and a wheezy piano stands in the corner. Daytime was given over to private lessons, conducted by the younger Otero, and presided over by the "original" Otero. Yes, there were two. The younger is the nephew and "star-pupil" of the great maestro who made dance history. The lesson begins. Everyone puts on castañuelas and begins to talk about something else, raising their voices over the clatter of three pairs of instruments. Both Oteros have corns on their thumbs worn by the cords. I often believe they forget to take them off when they go to bed! We are not talking about dancing. Young Mr. Otero is offering to have some special cigarettes made for me by one of his pupils who works in the tobacco factory. Old Otero is deploring the decline of the bullfight, and saying that he attends them no more, for all artistry has gone from them. The names of the great toreros slip from his tongue—Esportero, Massantini, and

later Belmonte, Chicuelo, Joselito..., and, he describes their perfection of line and their courage, until the dim hall is peopled with
color and beauty, and blood and death. Otero shakes his head sadly.
Nothing is what it once was. Nowadays he can't go to the theater
either, the dancing is so bad. Dancers have grown lazy, and fill their
routines with taconeo, instead of learning the old classical steps that
graced the Andalucian dance of his day. On request, Nephew Otero
executes a series of exquisite lazos. Uncle Otero shakes his head sadly.
He feels even his star pupil has gone off a bit. But this gets us around
to the fact that we are there to dance. The pianist strikes up. Nephew
Otero whirls through the first movement of a dance. Knowing his
system and having studied Spanish dancing for years, I manage to
catch the first few steps. "Which foot do I start on?" "It doesn't
matter."

But of course it does—as one finds on reaching the second step!
And let me say right here that going to Spain to study Spanish dancing is useless unless you have already a first class command of the
technique given you by someone who has studied abroad long enough
to know the importance of teaching technique before dances.

Our lesson goes on. Maestro José Otero corrects lines and effects—
sometimes the pupil, and sometimes the teacher, who, as far as he is
concerned, is still a boy-student. If you are so lucky as to have seen
an original copy of Otero's book, "Tratado de Bailes," you will see
in the illustrations a blond dancer with the naïve face of a choir-boy.
That is Nephew Otero, now a man of sixty-odd, and the greatest
teacher of the Spanish dance in the world today. For his teacher, the
greatest teacher of the Spanish dance the world has known, was
killed some years ago. The war? No. Burglars broke into his house.
He was past eighty, but he was Andalucian. He arose to protect his
property with his bare fists and they killed him.

But when I was there he was alive, very much so; his eye still
centered around the art for which he did so much. The lesson ends
suddenly. Otero remembers he was due over a half-hour ago at the
house of a grandee's daughter to whom he must give a private lesson
since she is not allowed the freedom of the studio. We talk a lot more,
and all leave together. On the street, we stop frequently to argue a
point. One can't gesture properly while walking. It sort of isn't
right, choreographically. Finally we part with greetings of "hasta la
noche" (until tonight) for I will be back at the studio in the evening,
which is the best time of all.

In the evening it is warm and there is a moon. A dozen pairs of castañuelas are sounding when we arrive. Dusty globes light the dusty
room. A typical orchestra of guitars, and bandurrias tune up in the

The Two Oteros (right) at a fiesta with their girls

corner. Fifteen or so girls of all ages move about the room, playing their palillos, while their parents sit on the wooden benches against the wall. The girls are in street dresses. They have come here straight from their work, for they are salesgirls, stenographers, tobacco-factory workers, seamstresses. They dance because they love it; because they are Andalucian. Every night they come here for two or three hours. They are unofficially known as "Otero's girls," and any fiesta, public or private, is graced by their dancing. Tonight they dance the Sevillanas, the Peteneras, the Tango de Cadiz, all the old favorites. Their eyes glow and their laughter rises. They have forgotten the weariness of their too-modern day. From time to time, Nephew Otero and the musicians slip into the patio for a glass of manzanilla; but, the old maestro needs no such stimulant with the dance before him. The session is long but nobody gets tired, not even the little child of seven with the gitana curl on her forehead, who spends her time between dances flirting outrageously with all the men present. Otero's neighbors drop in to add to the jaleo. Near midnight the girls reluctantly break it up out of respect for their workaday tomorrow. This happens every night, but no one ever gets tired of it, for this is Sevilla.

When the girls dance at fiestas they wear costumes. Bright ruffled organdies with colored scarves and fresh flowers. Five to a carriage, they ride in a little cavalcade down the streets of Sevilla through an avenue of "piropos" and gentle "olés." The greatest fiesta of the year is the week's celebration of the Cruz de Mayo. Everybody dances and sings all night and most of the day. The wrought-iron gates of the houses are thrown open, and the dancers, both town folk and gypsies, stroll from house to house making entertainment and receiving food and drink in return. It is a holiday strictly Sevillian, and celebrates the Feast of the Holy Cross—the finding of the Holy Cross by Santa Elena on May 3rd.

The Calle de la Sierpe is one of the many famous streets of Sevilla. It is an arcade running through a square, covered, and closed to wheeled traffic. Sidewalk cafés line it on both sides, and on a Sunday the Sevillian "chulos" meet to talk and to see—and to be seen. Nearly all of them wear the broad-brimmed "sombrero cordovez"; half wear "pantalon ceñido"; and, the real Beau Brummels wear the short jacket and ruffled shirt. Collars are considered inelegant. The shirt is fastened at the throat with a gold button. I shall never forget the resplendent figure of a chulo in full costume made in shepherd's check trimmed in black braid! He was fully aware that all feminine Sevilla was watching him.

On a Sunday Sevillian ladies wear high combs and mantillas, black for the married girls and white for the maidens, they say. They walk sedately, eyes on ground, the theory is that they are only going to or coming from mass. I wonder. Of course, in the afternoon there is the bullfight. Then the ladies take carriages to the bullring, a manton draped over the back of their vehicle. It is considered very rich if the fringes trail in the dusty street. When they arrive, the manton will be draped over the box-rail so that on the "sombra" (shade) side the half-circle presents a kaleidoscope of color. We always sit with the folk on the "sol" (sun) side, not to miss the spectacle of elegant, Sunday Sevilla! Happy the Sunday when a romantic scandal blooms under the impetus of a torero dedicating a bull to a famous beauty! This is a privilege of the bullfighter, and demands no forewarning. He merely steps up to the box and throws her his "felucca" (cap), which he does not wear while performing the "estocada." Perhaps the lady herself has had previous warning, perhaps the torero has sent one of his "cuadrilla" to her with his entrance cape, a brilliant satin affair not used for actually playing the bull. She drapes this over her box-rail, and awaits the moment when he will publicly dedicate the bull to her. Some of the afficionados recognize his cape, and the whispering starts. She holds his cap while he flirts with death. If the kill is well done, the public will award the torero the ear of the animal; if he has surpassed himself, two ears; if he has given them a rarely perfect performance, two ears and the tail! When he goes back to the box to receive the plaudits of his señorita, he may offer her the bloody trophy of his triumph.

All this happened to me once. I was in the public eye,—the visiting dancer—and there is something fatalistic about "dancer-meets-bull-fighter!" One evening after my concert, I met a handsome young bullfighter (they are all so young!) just starting his career. In fact, he was making his official debut the following Sunday. He offered me a box. When Sunday rolled around we were there in a front-line box, in the sombra this time! He sent me his green satin cape! What a thrill! I felt like Carmen as I draped it over the rail of the box! He killed his first bull cleanly and well, and the afficionados were agog. The great Spanish ballet moved on. The moment came for his second bull. He came before my box, and with a flourish, dedicated to me the great black monster pawing the sand a few yards away. I clutched the little round black hat. The boy was nothing to me but a name, a slim young artist giving a perfect performance. I knew very well that at bottom the dedication to me was a sort of "publicity stunt" for his debut. He was going well and wanted to do something dramatic to make the afficionados talk a lot about him. This "romantic scandal" would spread all over Spain! Yet for all that, I sat and

THE BULLFIGHTER (second from right)

clutched that hat in a spasm of nervousness, though half an hour before I had seen him face death and had applauded enthusiastically and impersonally. Now I held his hat, and that just changed everything! The ballet went on its rhythmic way, the slim boy and the great beast each doing his part. Then something slipped in the timing. Perhaps one was too bold or the other too clever. Suddenly I saw that silken, spangled body go hurtling through the air! I screamed! Of course I did! In the approved Carmen manner. I screamed without even knowing I had done it until it was all over and my friends teased me about it. He didn't seem hurt as he got up, dusty and somewhat torn (Heaven knows what sacrifice that now ruined "traje de luz" had cost him). But he was furious. His eyes glittered and his face went white. Barehanded he walked straight up to the bull and slapped its face! His nerves weren't even shaken, and he finished the performance so cleanly and perfectly that the afficionados awarded him both ears and tail! I still have the tail hung in my studio with "bandarillas" (barbs) and a capa. I never saw my torero again. He went to the hospital with smashed ribs right after the fight, and the next day I left to work in another town. I wonder where he is now; if he still lives in Sevilla, or if death found him; death from the bullet of a foe more crazed than the bull, and perhaps, less noble.

I used to go of evenings to the cafetins of Sevilla. I sat in one of the two or three tiers of boxes that line the hall. The pit is taken up with tables where only men sit, to drink and discuss everything, but mostly "the corrida and zapateado." In these cafetins have blossomed for over a century the adored tonadilleras. Carmen la Cigarrera, Rosa da Triana, then Amalia Molina, La Macarena and Pastora Imperio, La Argentina and Argentinita. When I was there the favorite was a beautiful young girl who was earnestly perfecting her dancing to follow the concert style. She was loved deeply and hopelessly by a handsome young Yankee who never missed an evening at the café where she danced. Young Otero was often present. Most of the artists had been his pupils, but he didn't go for that. He went for the manzanilla and the endless talk of the men. Old Otero never went, for "the dancing and singing isn't any good anymore." One evening the box next to us was occupied by a Sevillian couple who were entertaining a friend from the north of Spain. The Sevillians true to their birthright, were lost in enthusiasm for the canto Flamenco. Not so the Galician. The persistence with which the Sevillian tried to make his guest "see the light" was pathetic as well as funny. To no avail! The Galician finally went to sleep and left his hosts to shout their "olés" alone.

Early morning in Sevilla. A sky as blue and beautiful as mother-ofpearl in the clear air. It is coolish. After my bath the washwoman stops me in the hall to speak of a traje de cola of mine. Her eyes fill with tears as she claps her hands softly. "It is exactly like that of the divine Pastora Imperio!" she tells me. While I am dressing a street pianino rumbles up under our window which overlooks the square. The donkey pulling it drops his head in contemplation while his master begins to turn the handle. Of course, the music is a sevillanas. It always is. It is well before breakfast, but before the first copla is finished a little group of street gamins have formed in the plaza; the dance springs into life, line and counterline melting and glowing under the faded, dusty garments, while "bien parado!" cries out the group of old men watching. The day in Sevilla; it began with the dance and it ended with the dance. Does it still? Letters tell me life has changed little in Andalucia. If this be true, then they still begin and end the day with the sevillanas!

After Sevilla, Granada, of course! The great red Alhambra looks across a deep green canyon to the whitewashed Albaicin. Murcillo Laborda (first guitar teacher to Segovia) is a friend of the gypsies. He taught me how to approach them, to gain their sympathy. They were an interesting group, the ones who sang and danced. The "Capataz" was an enormous handsome woman dressed in white cotton printed with huge "lunares" (polka dots). La Mosca was the teacher. She was old now, but had once been the best of the gitana dancers. La Castillana was slim and blonde, and sang divinely the Cante Jondo. La Cagachina was tall and dark and beautiful. La Jardin, daughter of La Mosca was training to fill her mother's place as teacher. There were a half dozen others, each with her talent, each with her type. But the best of all was La Bisca. Curly red-blonde hair, a turned-up nose sprinkled with freckles, and gitana pura! What a dancer! There has never been anything like her. And yet Laborda told us that when she works on a stage half her fire goes, and she is no better than the others. No artist can remain impervious to the undisguised admiration of another artist. After I had gazed at La Bisca like a child at Santa Claus for a few hours, she couldn't help but like me.

Now *studying* with the gitana is practically impossible. First, they are extremely jealous of their arts. Second, I doubt if they learn "steps" in the sense that we do. "Steps" are probably born in them, or absorbed from childhood. One day in the cuevas the gitanas were dancing and I was questioning La Mosca about the different legends surrounding the dances. La Castillana was singing to guitar accompaniment of El Chico. But when I pulled out pencil and paper to note down some legendary lore, the music stopped and El Chico rose with

La Meri with Las Gitanas Del Sacro Monte (Granada)

a black face. He thought I was taking down in notes his improvised melodies. It took some convincing to bring him back, and although I never again produced pencil and paper in the cuevas, I don't think he ever quite trusted me. But I had to know. I *had* to know (it's a disease with me!) and, thanks to Laborda, I persuaded La Bisca to help me. It all had to be done in secret so the other gitanas wouldn't know, or they would have been furious. We arranged to meet at ten one morning in a cafetin we all knew. La Bisca was a little late. She came in a summer street dress and rolled stockings of the "flapper," her bobbed hair flying. The room was stale with the smoke of all-night patrons. Cigarette butts and spilled liquids filthied the floor. The piano was a miserable affair—and the pianist hadn't shown up. But La Bisca felt there was no use wasting time. "The alegrias goes like this...," she said, and she began to whistle and snap her fingers. The first five minutes I managed to ask whys and wherefores—after that we just did jaleo and enjoyed ourselves. She was a witch. I don't know what she did to us. I know I felt choked and there were tears in my eyes. La Bisca wasn't trying to create an effect. She would stop from time to time to explain things. I don't think anyone even heard her, for she had sent us away to another world which has nothing to do with common sense. Presently the nearly-blind pianist came in. No one greeted him, he just slipped over to the piano, watched her a moment, and began to play. Half the notes were gone off the crazy keyboard; he couldn't have seen the music even if he could read it, which I doubt. But he was Andalucian, and he played! We were four; Laborda, Carreras, my sister, myself. We made jaleo. Presently the jaleo grew louder, for along the balcony around the dance-floor, heads appeared. Who knows who inhabited those dusty bedrooms above the cheap café. The waiters? The dancing girls? Worse? I never knew and cared less. They had been up all night, but they had heard the bulerias, and their day had begun again. "Olé! Olé!" they shouted. La Bisca's eyes sparkled, and I think we were all slightly hysterical. She caught at my hand and pulled me up on the floor with her. I don't know what nor how I danced, and I didn't care. Neither did anybody else, for it was perfectly clear to all how I felt, and it's the feeling that counts in gitano dancing. I know I have never danced the baile Flamenco so perfectly before, or since, because that was the one time in my life when I had to dance, when the fear of death itself couldn't have kept me off that floor! And that's just what gypsy dancing must be!

Some days later I danced with the girls in the cueva for the delectation of some American tourists. Poor tourists, they didn't know it was me, and that I (for one) was "gypping" them!

LA ARGENTINA

In an ancient palace of a Moorish grandee lives La Tortajada. I called on her one evening. Her house is comfortable and awfully "gay nineties," Spanish be-ribboned mandolins hang in nooks; art-photographs adorn the walls; and everywhere is a profusion of bright paper flowers and of mantones de Manila. Someone inadvertently remarked that I was Protestant. La Tortajada instinctively drew back from me. But the feeling was momentary, for as she turned her great innocent eyes on me she asked, "Do tell me, do Protestants believe in God?" I told her yes. She seemed surprised and, pursuing the subject, asked if Christ and the Virgin were among our beliefs. She was amazed to hear they were.

Up a narrow cobbled street near the Alhambra is a quaint, old house with a simple garden. Here lived maestro Manuel De Falla. The great genius, old and sick, and working ceaselessly on his opera, received me. I wanted to talk about his visualization of his two great ballets, "El Amor Brujo" and "Sombrero de Tres Picos." Of the former he said that he had despaired of ever seeing it staged to his taste. Even the fine performance of La Argentina's group in Paris lacked some points in costuming and staging to make it perfect. I talked long with this great man—a rare privilege. They say that all during the recent conflict he sat quietly in his home in Granada, busy with his work, living in his own world in which the bitterness of war had no part.

The Moorish influence is so apparent in the art of the Granada gitanas, that I felt I had to go to Morocco and see the "grandmammy" of the "baile gitano." So I went from Granada to Fez and Marakesh and studied. It was my first material dip into undiluted Orientalism. I wish I could tell you about those ancient cities so unchanged by the changing centuries! But this book is about Spanish dancing. Morocco is the opening of another volume—a gateway to a road which leads to India, and Java and Japan.

The old epoch is closed. José Otero is dead. So is, surely, Doña Paulina. La Belle Otero walks sedately down the streets of Paris, her black eyes still melting in her now-wrinkled face. La Tortajada lives among the treasures of her triumphs in Granada. Pastora Imperio tours Spain. Amalia Molina—I saw her last in Caracas. What a woman! I would not be so indiscreet as to suggest her age. But she has the salero, the charm of a young girl. What *have* these Spanish women got? Her work is untouched by the classical renaissance. She is an embodiment of the theater of her time; the spangled tonadillera of twenty years ago. We hear no more from La Goya. Maria Montero is dead—and La Argentina.

I knew Argentina very slightly. I was traveling in New Zealand

Photo of La Meri by Marcus Blechman

"This book is for those of us who feel the call of Spain"

when I heard of her death. It shocked me profoundly, and I could think of nothing else for days. At my first performance after the news came through, five lines in a local newspaper—the requiem of so much beauty, I played the record, Granados No. 6, with an empty stage. Many of my audience did not know why, since she never appeared in Australasia. For her sake it was too late to teach them; but for the sake of the Spanish dance-art for which she gave her life, it was not.

Lately, the ultimate tragedy; we shall not see again the irreplaceable Argentinita lift her lovely head in Albeniz's "Triana," nor hear her light sweet voice in the "Jota." Elegant and intensively feminine, she possessed the delicate strength of a tempered Toledo blade. She was tireless in her striving for the perfection of her art both in her own performances, in her choreography, and in the research which gave strength to the dance-art of Spain. Her life was so consumed by her work that her very friendships were instinctively chosen for the contribution they might ultimately make to it. In the last years the weariness of long illness which must have consumed her body, never touched her spirit. Only once I heard her tell her mirrored self, "It isn't practice you need now, Argentinita—it's rest!"

She had planned one more tour of Spain before she retired to live and write among the trophies of her great glory.

Her death in New York almost on the very eve of her return to her beloved country, was an irreparable loss for she was the finest contemporary concert dancer of any idiom.

We are entering a new epoch; we are seeing the making of a new art-form. Because Otero and Argentina lived, every starry-eyed dancer in Andalucia tries to interpret the great music of her country and deplores her own lack of culture. It was not so in the old days. Today there is a choice. It isn't "dancer-meets-bullfighter" for all of them; many have heard the call of aspiration, and are giving all they have for the noblification of their art.

This book is written for those readers who in spite of their birthplace have in their heritage the deep insistent call of Spain. And to all those dancers, from the Andaluces delicias to Argentinita, who have conquered the world with their laughing castanets, we offer the incense of our gratitude, and dedicate this book, hoping all who read it will come a step nearer to understanding the passionate, rhythmic, hermetic soul of Spain.

Appendix

TECHNICAL
TERMINOLOGY

*A*lthough Spanish dancing has long possessed a terminology of its technique, it has not been crystallized into the printed word since 1716. The steps of the dance have been baptized by the folk, and they are appropriately descriptive. But naturally in many cases there is some difference of opinion on which name applies to which step. This is because the steps as well as the names somewhat overlap each other; and because the Spanish teacher seldom teaches as the ballet does, by isolated steps. Rather he teaches through dances, and hence uses the name of the step only as a reminder to the dancing pupil.

In compiling this appendix of the terminology in which I have reason to have faith, I give my authorities. I am fairly certain that there will be those who disagree. This is inevitable. But it is my hope that this first attempt to crystallize the terms of Spanish technique will result in corrections, additions and the eventual establishment of a terminology as complete and internationally understood as that of the Italian ballet.

Many of the terms, especially those applied to classic *steps* (as opposed to combinations) are universally recognized. These I have marked *cl.* (classic). Other terms are applied to combinations of steps; and when this combination is, so to speak, the theme-step of a traditional dance, the title of that dance is used to name the combination; for these are the names my teachers have shouted to me while teaching me dances. These terms I have marked *a.t.* (applied terminology).

In describing these steps, I have been as clear and simple as possible.

In this, like any other art, it isn't "what" but "how." The description is nearly useless to anyone who has not studied Spanish dancing, or has a flare for it amounting to genius. For each step is replete with a unique style; must have subtle knees, and contrasting arm and body-line. In indicating the arm movements (it is impossible to describe them fully!), I use the expression "opposing arms." I mean by this that if the *right* foot, or leg, is working, then the *left* arm is raised. In writing "circle from fifth," I mean that the arm starts from 5th position, lowers outward from the body, through 2nd position, as low as the waist, and then lifts in front of the body to return to fifth.

For convenience in reference I have listed the steps alphabetically. For convenience in learning them I have added a list which divides the steps described in the dictionary into four groups. Each group is more difficult than the one preceding it. The terms are listed in these groups more or less in order of their difficulty.

The authorities from whom I have gathered this terminology are the following:—

Pablo Minguet (from his book written in 1716)
José Otero of Sevilla, with whom I studied Andalucian
Doña Paulina of Barcelona, with whom I studied paysano
Carmen de Toledo, with whom I studied flamenco
Ortega of Madrid, with whom I studied classic
La Bisca of El Albaicin, and her sister gitanas
Curt Sachs' book "World History of the Dance"
Juan Martinez, in his published articles and private conversation.

AIRE—Air. Draw up the body.

ASSAMBLE (cl.)—To bring feet together in 3rd or 5th.

BACIO, EL (a. t.)—To lift the leg with bent knee; then straighten (not lock!) the knee. As Destaque in Dos Tiempos.

BACIO, en Vuelta (a. t.)—Hopping on L, execute bacios with R, turning towards R and en place.

BALANCEADO (cl.)—Step side R foot; L foot in back takes weight on half-toe; R takes weight en place.

BATIDO (cl.)—the lifted leg is struck against the other leg, or strikes it in passing in front or behind.

BATIMAN (cl.)—To lift the leg so that the foot is in front of the supporting ankle; move it to behind the ankle; straighten the knee to extend the foot to the side, oblique.

BIEN PARADO (cl.)—pose at end of copla; planta natural, weight on R, L forward, R arm up, L across.

BISCA, LA (a. t.)—With knees tightly together and bent, take very small steps forward. Swing knees from side to side.

BORNEAR—Bend; Twist.

BRISES (cl.)—As ballet.

BULERIAS (a. t.)—Stamp right foot en place; step right foot en place; step across right onto left; step right back. Repeated alternating. All is done with very small steps and with zarendeo.

BULERIAS CORRIDA (a. t.)—Same, but moving forward and all movements softer.

CABALLO (a. t.)—Step R en place; hop R en place; step L in front of R; step R en place; hop R en place; step L in back of R; step R en place; hop R en place; step L in front of R; step side R; step back L; step side R; step front L.

CABRIOLA (cl.)—Leap into air; extend R leg, beat L foot to R; return on L foot.

CABRIOLA CRUZADA (cl.)—As cabriola but beating ankle, or lower calves.

CABRIOLA TEXIDA (cl.)—As cabriola cruzada, but returning on R foot.

CACHUCHA (a. t.)—Campanela with the R; esplante to the R. Performed to ¾ tempe. The Campanela comes on the musical "and" to begin. The esplante takes the first bar and the first beat of the second bar. The second Campanela uses the "2"—"3" of the second bar. Opposing arms alternate circling from 5th.

CADENA (cl.)—R hand to R of partner and circle.

CAIDA (cl.)—Fall. Typical of Farruca.

CAMPANELA (a. t.)—Left thigh forward, lower leg vertical; swing lower leg side-wise.

CAREOS (cl.)—3 steps forward, (L, R, L); cross R over to make a vuelta por delante.

CARRERILLA (a. t.)—or CARRERITA—a run of short steps on the half-toe.

CARRETILLA—Roll of the castañuelas.

CEASE (cl.)—Step R to R side; bring L to R in 3rd or 5th position in front or back.

CONTRACEASE (cl.)—As cease, but alternating front and back.

CHIRIMEO (a. t.)—Same as "Lazos."

CONTINENZA (cl.)—Step side with a swaying shift of balance.

CORTADO (cl.)—(sometimes called CARGADO or TRONCO)—with the weight on the R, join the L to it, *immediately* taking the weight on the L.

CRUZADO (cl.)—Old style of cruzar por delante.

CRUZAR POR DELANTE (cl.)—Foot crossed in front over other ankle.

CRUZAR POR DETRAS (cl.)—Foot crossed behind at knee.

CUARTA (cl.)—jump into the air and move the R foot to behind the L, returning it to the original position before regaining the ground.

CUARTA CUADRADA (a. t.)—From 2nd position leap into the air. The R strikes the front of the L ankle, and moves to behind the L before one regains the floor in 5th position.

CUNA (cl.)—With feet crossed at ankles, take weight on alternate half-toes, produce rocking effect.

CUNA EN VUELTA (cl.)—Cuna turning.

DESPLANTE (Alegrias) (cl.)—L (one bar of ¾ tempe) R (2nd bar, 1 beat); L (2nd bar, 1 beat); point R twice en place and forward (2nd bar 1 beat and 3rd bar).

DESPLANTE (Bulerias) (cl.)—Flat stamps. R (one bar of ¾ tempe); L ("and" of 2nd bar); R ("1" of 2nd) twice L (2nd and 3rd counts of 2nd bar); R (3rd bar).

DESTAQUE (cl.)—From 5th position, lift front leg to side and lower it into 5th in back.

DESTAQUE EN DOS TIEMPOS (cl.)—As above, except leg lifts in two movements; the thigh lifts with lower leg vertical; then the lower leg straightens.

ECHADO (cl.)—To leap from one foot to the other.

EMBOTEADO (cl.)—Step back on R; hop on R, lifting L leg, knee to side, foot in front of R ankle, passes to in back of R ankle. Repeat alternating.

ENCAJE—Same as "Lazos."

ESCOBILLA (cl.)—Brush of half-toe. Used in flamenco and paysano dances.

ESCOBILLA CORRIDA (a. t.) Step R toward R oblique; swing L leg forward toward R oblique; touch L heel; touch L toe without changing position of L foot; step on L in position where it is. Repeat alternating.

ESPLANTE (a. t.)—Step side on R; point L forward in 4th, and take weight with it on the half-toe for the musical "and"; take weight with R en place. Repeat alternating. Opposing arms alternating circles from 5th.

ESTET (cl.)—Same as "Echado."

FILIGRANO (a. t.)—Soft movements in gitana work. Here the accent is on the arms.

FLOREO (cl.)—Lift L leg with the knee straight; bend the knee without moving the thigh.

FLORETA EN VUELTA (a. t.)—Floreta Passada; the last two steps are used to execute a Vuelta de Passo. Repeat alternating.

FLORETA NATURAL (a. t.)—Step forward L, make a Floreo with the R; step forward with R; bring to 3rd behind R. Repeat alternating to ¾ tempe the first step and the floreo take the first bar; the other two steps the second. Opposing arm alternated on 3rd or 4th.

FLORETA PASSADA (a. t.)—As Floreta Natural, except that the last step is forward instead of brought together.

GORGOLLATA (a. t.)—Step R on R; rodazan por adentro and a half-turn of the body; step L on L; rodazan with a half-turn of the body completing the turn. Opposing arms circle from 5th.

JALEO (a. t.)—Cross R tightly over L and take the weight on it; step L en place across R again, taking weight; lift L leg up in back from knee.

JEREZANA (a. t.)—Point R 3rd in front; lift R leg up in back from knee.

JEREZANA, PASO DE (cl.)—Point R 4th in front; lift R leg up in back from knee; step R forward; L forward, making a half-turn of body to right; touch R foot to L arch; lift R leg in media rodazan.

JEREZANA CORRIDA (a. t.)—A jerezana followed by two steps forward. Repeat alternating.

JEREZANA EN VUELTA (a. t.)—Step on L; point R forward in 4th; lift R backward from knee, at the same time executing quick turn en place.

JOTA (a. t.)—Jump in to matalaraña, spring into air, extending R leg to side (not high, and very straight); pas de buret natural. The arms are in 6th.

LAZOS (cl.)—On the half-toe, step forward from 3rd (L forward) to 3rd (R forward, passing the feet around each other by turning out the heels. Executed both forward and backward.

LLAMADA (a. t.)—Weight on L, beat R in 3rd and in 2nd (see page 69).

MALAGUEÑAS (a. t.)—Step R on R; L points in 3rd before R; step L on L; R points in 3rd before L; raise R leg in Campanela and put it down in back of L. Opposing arms work from 4th to 4th. Repeat alternating ⁶⁄₈ tempe, one movement on each count.

MANCHEGAS (a. t.)—Cease; echado onto R; step back L; R point in 3rd forward; R rodazan and down in back of L. The cease is executed on the musical "and l." There is one count to each of the other movements. Opposing arms alternate in 4th position.

MARIANAS (a. t.)—Feet together in 1st; jump to R; jump to L; jump back.

MATALARAÑA (cl.)—Leap into air and return with weight on L, and R pointed to R oblique.

MENEO (a. t.)—Bend knees.

MORISCA (a. t.)—A jerk of the body originating in the backbone just above the waist, and snapping the whole, loosely-held, upper torso.

OLÉ (a. t)—Stamp R en place; point L to 2nd and take weight on half-toe; step R en place. Repeat alternating. Executed with zarendeo of the hips.

OLÉ EN VUELTA (a. t.)—Same, turning en place.

PALMADAS—Hand claps.

PANADEROS (a. t.)—Step side-oblique on R; step L front of R; step side-oblique on R; step L in back of R; step side-oblique on R; campanela with L. Repeat alternating. (I find this step peculiarly difficult to reduce to understandable terms. The opposing movement of the upper body controls the legs in a certain way to create an unique swing.) Opposing arms alternate in 3rd position. In ⅜ with one movement to each count.

PANADEROS EN VUELTA (a. t.)—Same turning en place.

PARADITAS (cl.)—Heels together; toes together; repeat da capo. With this movement, progress sidewise.

Parado—See "Bien Parado."

Pasada—Step forward R; step forward L; step forward R at the same time execute a half-turn with the body; step back L; point R in 3rd front; campanela R. One movement to each count. Arms in 5th, R arm circles from 5th.

Pas De Buret Detras (cl.)—L steps 3rd in front of R; R steps back oblique; L step 3rd in front.

Pas De Buret Natural (cl.)—(Often called simply Pas de Buret) L steps down in 5th behind R; R, a small step side; L, 5th in front of R.

Pas De Buret Por Delante (cl.)—L to 3rd in back; R forward R oblique; L 3rd in back.

Paseo De Alegrias (a. t.)—Step R oblique with R, lifting thigh with bent knee; cortado with L; repeat both movements. (The same term is applied to several different forms of filigrano used in the Alegrias.)

Paseo De Las Palmas (a. t.)—Jerezanas Corridas executed in a circle with accompanying palmadas.

Paso De Vasco (cl.)—Echado on R; slide L to R oblique past R; cortado R. Repeat alternating. Opposing arms circle from 5th.

Paso De Vasco En Vuelta (cl.)—Waltz turns.

Pasodoble (cl.)—Simple, gliding pas de basque.

Paso Ondulado (a. t.)—Any gitano step taken flowingly, without taconeo, and with much filigrano.

Paso Sencillo (cl.)—Step.

Peteneras (a. t.)—Step forward R; point L to 4th forward, and lift L in floreo; four steps forward, beginning with L. Each step takes one count. The point and campanelas together take one count.

Pica (a. t.)—Strike the ball of the foot on the ground with an audible thud (a part of taconeo).

Piflac (cl.)—Echado onto the R across the L; the L finishes in cruzar por delante. Execute a turn during these movements.

Pito (a. t.)—Snapping of fingers.

Planta Cuadrada (cl.)—A leap into 2nd position.

Planta Natural (cl.)—A static pose. Weight on the R with the L slightly in advance.

Puntapie (cl.)—Kick.

Punta Y Talon (a. t.)—Point toe in 2nd (heel upwards); point R heel in 2nd.

Rastron (cl.)—Glide.

Redoble (a. t.)—
Right	Left	Right	Left
Stamp	Stamp	Toe-heel	Heel-stamp

Redoble Flamenco (a. t.)—
Left	Right	Left	Right	Left
Stamp	Stamp	Stamp	2 Stamps	Stamp

Retortilles (cl.)—Same as paraditas.

RETORTILLES, MEDIA (cl.)—Step R to side; heel-toe L.

RETORTILLES POR DETRAS—Retortilles moving backward.

REVERENCIA CORTADA (cl.)—Bacio R, and put it down behind L; bend body a little jump onto R.

RIPIQUETEO (a. t.)—Right　　　　or　　　　Left
　　　　　　　Heel-stamp　　　　　Heel-stamp

RIPRESA (cl.)—from 4th, weight on front foot; sway back and draw front foot back to 3rd.

RODAZAN (cl.)—A complete circle of lower leg without disturbing thigh.

RUEDA (cl.)—Small circle.

SACADO (cl.)—Weight on R; L performs cortado; R immediately steps R oblique.

SALERITO (cl.)—A pass in the Sevillanas.

SALERITO (a. t.)—Same as "Rodazan."

SALIDA (cl.)—Entrance. Preparatory steps.

SALTILLO (cl.)—Hop (old style)—skip.

SALTO (a. t.)—Same as "Echado."

SALTO Y CAMPANELA (a. t.)—Leap R; L swings past R to form campanela forward. Repeat alternating.

SEVILLANAS (a. t.)—Step forward R; L point in 3rd behind; step back L; point R 3rd in front; bacio R; step R en place. Repeat alternating. Opposing arms alternate 4th position (see page 66).

SEVILLANAS, MEDIA (a. t.)—Step side R; touch L in 3rd behind R; touch L in 4th behind R.

SOBRESUT (cl.)—Same as matalaraña, save that the legs are lifted high *in back* from the knees.

SOSTENIDO (cl.)—Weight on one foot, the other pointed.

SOSTENIDO DOS PIEDS (a. t.)—On the half-toe, weight on both feet.

TACO (a. t.)—Stab floor with heel.

TACONEO (a. t.)—Any heel work.

TANGO (a. t.)—Step R; step forward L; cortado R; Repeat alternating. In two-fourth; the first step takes two counts; the other two, one each.

TANGO EN VUELTA (a. t.)—Tiempo di tango turning en place.

TIEMPO DI TANGO (a. t.)—Step side R; L back, 4th; R stamp en place. Execute in the same tempe as the tango step.

TRONCO (cl.)—Coupe; cut.

VALONÉ (cl.)—Swing leg across in front of sustaining leg.

VUELTA CON TIJERA (cl.)—Kick left forward, hopping on R; before returning to ground, kick R forward, returning to ground on L (hitch-kick); R foot down and front of L to execute a vuelta por delante.

VUELTA DA PASO (a. t.)—Step R; step L with a half-turn of body toward R; step L completing turn toward R.

VUELTA DE LLAMADA (a. t.)—With weight on R, point L to 3rd and 2nd (or 4th and 2nd) turning the body toward R en place.

VUELTA DE PECHO (cl.)—Valone R; step side R; vuelta volada.

VUELTA DE PIRUETA (cl.)—Step side oblique onto R; step onto L, swinging body entirely around and at the same time bringing the R up on front of the L knee, or ankle.

VUELTA DE RIÑON (cl.)—Lift L leg forward; circle from hip-joint to back; put down in back of R to make a vuelta por detras with quebrada.

VUELTA DE TORNILLO (cl.)—From 5th position; turn completely round finishing in 5th.

VUELTA EN CUATRO TIEMPOS (cl.)—Four little steps en place make one complete turn.

VUELTA POR DELANTE (cl.)—Step R; cross L over closely; turn shortly and finish in planta natural.

VUELTA POR DETRAS (cl.)—Place R foot back in close 4th, rise on balls and pivot slowly.

VUELTA QUEBRADA (cl.)—Cross R over L, bending body forward at waist; turn body slowly, bending from waist to R, then to L. The effect of this turn is that the audience continually sees the crown of the dancer's head.

VUELTA QUEBRADITA (a. t.)—Vuelta por delante, but with foot crossed into 4th, and the body bent at the waist on one side. (Step R; cross L in 4th; bend toward L at waist, and turn.)

VUELTA VOLADA (cl.)—Step side R; echado onto L, making complete turn to R.

VUELTA VOLADA TEXIDA (cl.)—As vuelta volada, but with R leg beating L while in air.

VUELTA ZAPATEADA (a. t.)—Weight on the R; pivot slowly toward R by executing picas with the L at 3rd and 4th back.

ZAPATEADO—Rhythmic patterns with the feet. Taconeo refers rather to the sharp noisy steps mostly with the heels. Zapateado includes this *and* the softer, brushing steps included in the filigrano.

ZARANDEO—Body movement. Hip swinging and the characteristic shaking of the shoulders.

GLOSSARY OF TERMS

Aficionado: fan
Agitanado: gypsy-ized
Albaicin: gypsy quarter of Granada
Alegre: happy
A lo alto: aristocratic
Alpargatas: roped-soled sandals
Alta danza: "high dance"; leaped dance
Andaluces delicias: Andalucians; girl dancers from the region of Andalucia
Argentina, La: stage name of Antonia Mercé
Argentinita, La: stage name of Encarnacion Lopez
Asentao: "seated"; serene or immobile torso

Bailador: male dancer
Bailarina: female dancer
Baile: dance; folk or figure dances
Bandarillas: barbs
Barrigas: trills
Barrio: quarter
Basse-dance: low dance; stepped, not jumped
Batterié, Fr.: beaten steps
Bien parado: well-posed
Brazeo: arm-carriage

Cadena: chain
Cafetin: small café
Caida: fall
Cale: gypsy
Camada rodoña: round kick

Camadas: leg swings or kicks
Cambré, Fr.: sway-backed
Cañades: gypsy quarter; see cañi
Cañi: gypsified (more particularly, gypsies from Galicia)
Cante jondo: literally, "deep song"; applied to gypsy songs
Capa: cape
Capataz: foreman; overseer
Carretillas: trills
Castaña: chestnut
Castañuelas: castanets
Chaquetilla: short jacket
Charros: Salamancans
Chinchines: crotals; tiny cymbals attached to fingers
Chocolate a la canela: a liquid chocolate, very, very thick and cinnamon-flavored
Chulos: Rakes; young loungers, very elegantly dressed, with, seemingly nothing to do but hang around cafés
Comicos: literally, "comics"; generally applied to actors
Copla: verse of song; or the music which is equivalent to same
Corazon: heart
Corrida: bullfight
Couplets: two-line verses which are sung
Cuadrilla: a group of four toreros attached to and supported by each "star" bullfighter

168APPENDIX

Cuadro flamenco: a scene in which a group of gypsies take turns at dancing typical dances, interspersed with gypsy songs
Cuevas: caves; habitations of the gypsies

Danza: dance; court dance
Desafío: challenge
Dueña: female chaperon

Entrada: entrance
Ersatz, Ger.: substitute
Espadrilles: rope-soled sandals
Espinillo: hard wood of the acacia family
Estilo di canto: style of singing
Estocada: sword-thrust which kills the bull
Estranjero: foreigner

Fea y contrahecha: ugly and misformed
Felucca: bullfighter's cap
Fin de fiesta: musical comedy pieces often followed by an "act" of dancing unrelated to the piece
Flamenco: gypsy; more particularly one who inhabits Triana in Sevilla
Folía: madness
Fonda: sidewalk café

Gaditana: female gypsy
Girates: turns
Gitana pura: pure gypsy
Gitanerias: pertaining to gypsies, gypsy quarters
Gitano: gypsy; more particularly one who inhabits Albaicin in Granada
Golpe de pie: Stamp of the foot
Grenadilla: hard wood similar to African blood-wood
Grito: cry; shout

Habas Verdes: green beans
Hasta la noche: until tonight
Herredores: fiestas
Huevo: hollow

Indiot: peacock

Jaleo: Combination of shouts, handclaps and foot-taps with which the watcher of the gypsy dance takes part in the general excitement
Juergas: parties
Juramento: oath

Leilas: Moorish song and dance festivals
Liso: solo; alone
Lunares: polka-dots

Madroño: net of chenille balls
Mantilla: oblong of lace worn over the head. In the old days smaller and triangular
Manton de Manila: an embroidered shawl. So-called because early Spanish mariners brought them home from Manila, when that city was a Spanish province. The shawls are actually made in China
Manzanilla: strong, bitter wine
Mas cañi de todos: most gypsy of all
Mas saltadora: more leaped
Matador: killer of the bull
Mauresque: the spiral in which all lines of motions return to the center force
Merceria: notion shop
Merengue: sweet
Monjes: monks
Montaracias: mountaineers
Monterra: snood
Morisco, a la: Moorish style
Muiño: mill

Natya: Sanskrit; science of dance drama
Navaje: long knife typical of Sevilla

Olé: cry of encouragement or approval (from "Allah")
Orejas: holes

Palillo: Andalucian term for castañuelas
Palmadas: hand-claps
Panadero: tambourine
Pantalon ceñido: long trousers tight at hip, waist, and ankle
Parado: pose
Patagueya: salute (Basque)
Patio: inner garden around which the house is built
Pasamano: grand right and left
Paseo di gracia: walk on and around stage; inimitably Spanish
Pas réglés, Fr.: regulated steps
Pavo: peacock
Paysano: peasant
Peineta: comb
Piropo: compliment
Pito: finger-snap
Por chufla: for a joke; satiric
Por lo fino: aristocratically
Postizos: Valencian term for castañuelas
Puente: bridge
Pulgaretes: Aragonese term for castañuelas

Reina: queen
Reyes Catolicos, los: Catholic kings; Ferdinand and Isabella
Ritmos: rhythms
Robado: alternating solos

Salero: pep; sex appeal; neither and both; typically Spanish

Salida: entrance
Serios: serious
Sol: sunny; sun
Sombra: shady; shadow
Sombrero cordobez: felt or pressed beaver hat (see page 118)
Sombrero de queso: "cheese hat," so-called because of its shape, velvet
Sotar: jump
Suertes: luck, applied to certain figures of the bullfight
Sudras: caste of Hindu craftsmen

Taconeo: heel-work
Tauramargie: pertaining to the technique of the bullfight
Tonadilla: popular song
Tonadillera: Spanish equivalent of the song-and-dance artist
Torero: bullfighter, (there is no such thing as a toreador outside opera)
Traje corto: man's costume
Traje de cola: tailed-dress, woman's dress with trail
Traje de luz: luxury costume; the elaborate costume of the bullfighter
Trencato: broken; or quick shuffling of the feet
Triana: gypsy quarter of Sevilla

Vaquero: cowboy of Asturia
Variedades: varieties
Villancico: stage sketch
Volar: fly

Zapateado: rhythmic patterns of heel, ball and sole of foot
Zarzuela: musical comedy
Zarzuelita: one act zarzuela

TABLE OF DANCES MENTIONED IN TEXT

NAME OF DANCE	PROVINCE	TYPE	PROBABLE ORIGIN	REMARKS
Agudillo	Burgos	Couple	Seguidillas	
Agudo	Burgos	Couple	Seguidillas	
A La Pandera	Burgos	Couple	Seguidillas	
Alegrias	Andalucia (Flamenco)	Solo	Song of Same Name	
A Lo Alto	Burgos	Couple	Seguidillas	
A Lo Bajo	Burgos	Couple	Similar to Agudo	
A Lo Grave	Burgos	Couple	Similar to Agudo	
A Lo Ligero	Burgos	Couple	See Agudo	
A Lo Llano	Burgos	Couple	Similar to Agudo	
A Lo Pecado	Burgos	Couple	Similar to Agudo	
Al Pandero	Burgos	Couple	Seguidillas	
Al Paran	Burgos	Couple	Similar to Agudo	
Ampurdanes	Catalunya	Round	Sardana	Same as Sardana but Starting to the Left
				District of Ampurdanes
Aquiera Villa				See Xaquera Vella
Arenilla	Valencia	Couple		
Arin-Arin	Basque	Couple	Jota Aragonesa	

171

TABLE OF DANCES MENTIONED IN TEXT (*Continued*)

NAME OF DANCE	PROVINCE	TYPE	PROBABLE ORIGIN	REMARKS
Arriba	Burgos	Couple	Seguidillas	
Aubada	Catalunya	Group of Men	Gallega	
Aurresku	Basque	Group	Pagan	Ritualistic
Baila	Galicia	Couple	Gallega	
Baila De La Reposa	Asturia	Round		
Bailao, El	Leon	Couple	Charrada	
Baile Corredo	Leon	Couple	Giraldella	Wedding Dance
Baile De La Manzana	Toledo	Group	Pagan Ritual	Danced at Weddings
Baile De Las Nyacras	Catalunya	Mixed Group	Greek	Dancers Play on Oyster Shells
Baile De Los Pollos	Asturia	Couple	Fandango	
Baile De Pandero	Asturia	4 or 5 Couples	Vaquero	
Bal Cerda	Catalunya	Group	Ballet De Deu and Ball Pla	Known also as Ball Dels Aranyous and Ball Rodo
Ball De Palau	Catalunya	Group	Greek	
Ball De La Teya	Catalunya	Group	Ancient Sacrificial Dance	
Ball De Llet	Catalunya	Group	Ancient Fertility Dance	
Ball Dels Aranyous	Catalunya, North	Group	Ballet De Deu and Ball Pla	

Dance	Region	Formation	Related Dance	Notes
Ball De Moixent	Valencia	Group	Xaquera Vella	
Ball De Torrent	Valencia	Group	Xaquera Vella	
Ballet	Catalunya	Couple	Ball De Palau	
Ballet De Deu	Catalunya	2 Lines of Men Dancers	Ball De Palau	
Ball Pla	Catalunya	Couple	Ball De Palau	
Ball Rodo	Catalunya (Barcelona)	Group	Ballet De Deu and Ball Pla	Known also as Ball Dels Aranyous
Bolangera	Catalunya	Round	Folk	Originated in the 14th Century
Bolangera	Valencia	4 Couples	Old Brandes or Ruedas	
Boleras De Los Gallegos	Galicia	Group or Couples	Bolero and Jota	
Boleras De Sequeros	Salamanca	Couple	Boleras De Los Gallegos	
Bolero	Castile	Couple	Chacona and Zarabanda via Cachucha	
Bollo, El	Salamanca	Couple	Charrada	Figures at Weddings and Fiestas
Brincandillas	Burgos	Couple	Seguidillas	
Bulerias	Andalucia (Flamenco)	Solo		
Cachucha	Castile	Couple	Zarabanda and Chacona	

TABLE OF DANCES MENTIONED IN TEXT (*Continued*)

NAME OF DANCE	PROVINCE	TYPE	PROBABLE ORIGIN	REMARKS
Capeo	Valencia	Couple	Mallorca	
Careado	Asturia	Couple	2nd Movement—Fandango	
Castaña, La	Catalunya	Couple		
Chacona	Extremadura	Couple	Basque	Called also Ratrojo or Villano
				Similar to Castilian Fandango
Chaconne	See Chapter III, 22, 23	Couple	Olé Gaditane	
Charrada, La	Salamanca	Couple	Seguidillas	
Chun-Chun	Navarra	Couple	Jota Aragonesa	
Cinta, La	Castile	Couple	Variation on the Dulzaina	
Contrapas	Catalunya	Round	Monks of Ariente	Very like the Sardana
Contrapaso	Galicia	Group or Couples	Muiñeira	
Corranda	Catalunya	Couple		Acrobatic in Style
Corri-Corri	Asturia	1 Man and 2 Women	Pagan Fertility Rites	
Corro	Leon	Round		
Danses, The	Catalunya	1 Man and 2 Women		
Danseas	Valencia	Round	Phoenician	

174

Danza	Valencia	Couple	Jota Valenciana	
Danza de Casamiento, La	Andalucia (Flamenco)	Solo and Group	Orient	Wedding Dance
Danza De La Magdalena	Asturia	Round	Danza Prima, La	
Danza De Los Huertanos, La	Valencia	Couple	Jota Valenciana	
Danza De San Pablo	Asturia	Round	Danza Prima, La	
Danza De San Pedro	Asturia	Round	Danza Prima, La	
Danza De San Roque	Asturia	Round	Danza Prima, La	
Danza Prima, La	Asturia	Round	Greek	
Dulzaina, La	Avila	Couple	Boleras De Los Gallegos	
Eixida	Catalunya	Couple		
Entradillo	Leon	Solo and Couple		Danced in Coplas
Fandango	Castile	Couple	Phoenician	
Fandango Punteado	Asturia	Couple	Similar to Baile De Pandero	
Fandanguillo	Andalucia	Couple	Sevillanas	
Fandanguillo	Murcia	Couple	Andalucia	
Farandole	Catalunya	Group	French Court	
Farruca	Andalucia (Flamenco)	Solo	Gitano Faico	
Folias	Valencia	Group	Greek	Festival Street Dance
Furioso, El	Valencia	Couple	Jota	

TABLE OF DANCES MENTIONED IN TEXT (*Continued*)

NAME OF DANCE	PROVINCE	TYPE	PROBABLE ORIGIN	REMARKS
Gala Gambeto	Catalunya	Round	La Gala.	
Gala, La	Catalunya	Solo or Group	Feudal Customs	
Gallegada	Galicia	Couple	Greek	
Garrotin	Andalucia (Flamenco)	Solo or Couple		
Geringosa	Asturia	Couple	A Lo Llano—Burgos	
Giraldilla	Leon	Couple	Giraldilla of Asturia	
Giraldilla	Asturia	Couple	2nd Movement of the Careado	
Guajiras, Las	Andalucia	Couple	Sevillanas	
Habas Verdes	Extremadura	Couple	Seguidillas	Also Danced in Salamanca
Hoe Dance	Basque	Solo	Ritualistic	
Huertana, La	Murcia	Couple	Greek	
Indiot	Catalunya	Square	Greek	
Jaleo	Andalucia	Couple	Sevillanas	
Jerezana, La	Andalucia	Couple	Sevillanas of Jerez	
Jota	Aragon	Couple		
Jota Al Aire	Catalunya	Couple	Jota Aragonesa	Similar to Corranda
Jota Aragonesa	Aragon	Couple	Basque or Canary Island	
Jota Extremeña	Extremadura	Couple	Basque	
Jota of Oviedo	Asturia	Couples	Jota Aragonesa	

176

Dance	Region	Formation	Description	
Jota Valenciana	Valencia	Couple	Jota Aragonesa	
Jotilla	Burgos	Couple	Similar to Agudo	
L'Hereu Riera	Catalunya	Man's Solo	Sword Dance	Danced over Crossed Sticks
Magosto	Galicia	Couple	Similar to Muiñeira Gallega	Similar to Sevillanas
Malagueña	Andalucia	Couple	Malaga	
Malagueña	Murcia	Couple	Andalucia	
Manchegas, Las	Andalucia	Couple	Castile	
Marianas	Andalucia	Solo	Flamenco	
Marratxes, Les	Catalunya	Group	Ancient Fertility Dance	
Milan	Burgos	Couple	Seguidillas	
Mocador	Catalunya	4 Couples	Orient	
Molleras, Las	Andalucia	Couple	Sevillanas	
Muiñeira Gallega	Galicia	Group or Couples	Celtic, Greek, Brigantinos	
Murciana	Murcia	Couple	Sauts-Basque	
Multidanzak	Navarra	Round	Olé Gaditane	
Olé, El	Andalucia	Woman's Solo	Las Andaluces Delicias	
Olé, Gaditane	Andalucia	Solo	Fandango	
Panaderos, Las	Andalucia	Couple	Fandango	
Pancha Corra	Zamora	Men and Women in 2 Lines		

TABLE OF DANCES MENTIONED IN TEXT (*Continued*)

NAME OF DANCE	PROVINCE	TYPE	PROBABLE ORIGIN	REMARKS
Pandaretes, Las	Valencia	Couple	Jota	
Pardica	Murcia	Round	Similar to Parranda	
Parilla	Burgos	Couple	Similar to Agudo	
Parranda	Murcia	Round	Greek	Danced in Coplas
Pasan	Burgos	Couple	Seguidillas	
Pasacalle	See Chapter II, 8	Couple	Moorish	
Pasiegas, Las	Santander	Men and Women in 2 Lines	Fertility Rites	Danced also in Quepuzco, Zamora, Aragon, Valencia, Murcia.
Passepied	See Chapter II, 8	Couple	Pasacalle	
Pavane	See Chapter III, 21	Couple		
Pericote	Asturia	1 Man and 2 Women		
Perlindango	Asturia	Couple	Giraldilla	
Peseta, La	Castile	Couple	Variation on the Dulzaina	
Peteneras	Andalucia	Solo	Seguidillas Sevillanas— Flamenco	
Polo Gitano	Andalucia (Flamenco)	Solo		
Porro	Catalunya	Group	Ancient Fertility Dance	
Ramose, Los	Extremadura	Group	Toledo	Wedding Dance
Rapsodia, La	Valencia	Couple	Jota	

Name	Region		Formation	Notes
Rebudixu	Asturia	Orient	Couples	
Romalis	Andalucia (Flamenco)	Olé Gaditane	Solo	
Rondeña		Fandango	Couple	
Rosca, La	Salamanca	Charrada	Couple	Figures at Weddings and Fiestas
Ruedas	Burgos	Ancient Ritual	Circle—Girls	Danced during Lent
Salton	Asturia	Fandango	Couple	
Sarabande	Castile	Zarabanda	Couples	
Sardana	Catalunya	Greek	Round	
Sauts-Basque	Basque	Branle	Group—Men and Women	Ritualistic
Seguidillas	Castile	Fandango	Couple	
Seguidillas Boleras	Castile	Seguidillas—Bolero	Couple	
Seguidillas Manchegas	Castile (La Mancha)	Cachucha	Couple	
Seguidillas Sevillanas	Andalucia	Seguidillas Manchegas	Couple	
Selvata	Catalunya	Sardana	Round	Same as Sardana but Starting to the Right—District of Selvata
Sevillanas	Andalucia	Seguidillas Manchegas	Couple	
Sevillanas Boleras	Andalucia	Seguidillas Manchegas	Couple	
Soleares	Andalucia (Flamenco)	Song of Same Name	Solo	
Sorongo	See Chapter II, 8	Moorish	Solo	

TABLE OF DANCES MENTIONED IN TEXT (*Continued*)

NAME OF DANCE	PROVINCE	TYPE	PROBABLE ORIGIN	REMARKS
Sword Dance	Basque	Solo	Spring Festival Ritual	
Tango	Andalucia (Flamenco)	Woman's Solo		
Tango de Cadiz	Andalucia	Solo	José Otero	
Tarara	Valencia	Couple	Castile	
Valenciana, La	Valencia	Couple	Jota Valenciana	Similar to Jota Valenciana
Vito	Andalucia	Woman's Solo	Flamenco	
Xaquera Vella	Valencia	Lines of Couples	Greek	One of the Oldest Dances of Spain
Xirenguelo	Asturia	4 or 5 Couples	Fandango	
Zambra	Andalucia (Flamenco)	Woman's Solo	Moorish	
Zandango	Castile (Valladolid)	Men and Women in 2 Lines	Gallegada	
Zangano	Murcia	2 Women and 1 Man	Greek	
Zapateado	Andalucia (Flamenco)	Man's Solo		
Zarabanda	See Chapter II, 8	Solo or Couple	Near Eastern	
Zortzico Vasconado	Basque	Solo	Movement of Aurresku	

BIBLIOGRAPHY

Acevedo y Huelves, Bernardo: "Vaqueros de Alzada in Asturias," imprenta del Hospicio Provincial Oviedo, 1893.

Anderson, Ruth: "Pontevedra and La Coruña," Hispanic Society of America, 1939, New York.

Beaumont, Cyril W.: "Fanny Elssler," C. W. Beaumont, 1931, London.

Bercovici, Konrad: "Story of the Gypsies," Cosmopolitan Book Corporation, 1928, New York.

Bolitho, William: "Twelve Against the Gods," Simon and Schuster, 1929, New York.

Borrow, George: "The Bible in Spain," Collins Clear Type Press, 1842.

Brown, Irving: "Deep Song," Harper Bros., 1929, New York.

Busquets, Llobet: "Bailes Tipicos y Escudos de España y sus Regiones," Raurich, 1929, Barcelona.

Calderon, Estebanez: "El Solitario" (Escenas Andaluzas), imprenta de W. Perez Dubrui, Colecion Escritores Castellanos, 1883, Madrid.

Calderon, Juan Jacinto Rodriguez: "Boleroguia," impreso en Philadelphia por Zacarias Pulson, 1807.

Capmany, Aurelio: "El Baile y La Danza" (Volume II, Folklore y Costumbres de España), Casa Editorial, Alberto Martin, 1934, Barcelona.

Carreras y Candi: "Folklore y Costumbres de España," Casa Editorial, Alberto Martin, 1934, Barcelona.

Charbonnel, Raoul: "La Danse," Garnier Frères, 1899, Paris.

Charteris, Leslie: "Juan Belmonte," Doubleday, 1937, Garden City, New York.

Chase, Gilbert: "Music of Spain," W. W. Norton and Co., Inc., 1941, New York.

Chavarre, Eduardo Lopez: "Popular Spanish Music," Editorial Labor, 1927, Barcelona-Buenos Aires.

Cheney, Sheldon Warren: "The Theater," Tudor Pub. Co., 1935, New York. Longmans, Green and Co., 1936, London.

Davies, John Langdon: "Dancing Catalans," Jonathan Cape, 1929, London.

Dictionnaire de Trevour, 1721.

Duff, Donald: "Flamenco," in Modern Music, May-June, 1940.

Ellis, Havelock: "The Dance of Life," The Modern Library, 1923, New York. "The Soul of Spain," Houghton Mifflin Co., 1909, Boston

Frazer, James: "The Golden Bough," Macmillan, 1922, New York.

Fuertes y Piqueras, Mariano Soriano: "Music Arabe-Española," J. Oliveres, impresor de S. M., 1853, Barcelona.

Gallop, Rodney: "The Book of the Basques," Macmillan and Co., Ltd., 1930, London.

Horst, Louis: "Pre-Classic Dance-Forms," The Dance Observer, 1940, New York.

Inzenga y Castillanos: "Bailes y Cantos Populares de España," A Romero A., 1888, Madrid.

Irving, Washington: "The Alhambra," Ginn and Co., 1915, New York.

Isaacson, Charles: The Dance Magazine, ca. 1925.

Kinney, Troy and Margaret West: "The Dance," Frederick Stokes, 1914, New York.

Levinson, André: "Argentina," Editions des Chroniques du Jour, 1928, Paris.

Minguet, Pablo e Irol: "Breve Tratado de los Passos," (El Danzado a la Española), 1737, Madrid.

Morand, Paul: "Spring in Spain," in Vogue Magazine, 1931.

Navarro, Juan Esquivel: "Discurso Sobre el Arte del Danzado," impreso en Sevilla en 1642 por Juan Gomez de Blas.

Oesterley, W. O. E.: "The Sacred Dance," Cambridge University Press, 1923.

Otero, José: "Tratado de Bailes," Guia Oficial, 1912, Sevilla.

Palencia, Isobel de: "El Traje Regional de España" B. T. Batsford, Ltd., 1926, London.

Reboux, Paul: "Teresina," Souvenir Program, 1932.

Rennert, Hugo Albert: "Spanish Stage in the Time of Lope de Vega," The Hispanic Society of America, 1909, New York.

Ribera, Julian: "Music in Ancient Arabia and Spain," Stanford University Press, 1929, California.

Rice, Cyril: "Dancing in Spain," British Continental Press, 1931, London. "Escudero," Souvenir Program.

Sachs, Curt: "World History of the Dance," W. W. Norton and Co., Inc., 1937, New York.

Smith, Laura Alexandrine: "Through Romany Songland," 1889, David Stott.

Starkie, Walter: "Spanish Raggle-Taggle," John Murray, 1934, London. "Don Gypsy," E. P. Dutton and Co., Inc., 1937, New York.

Vechten, Carl Van: "The Music of Spain," Alfred A. Knopf, 1918, New York.

Vuillier, Gaston: "La Danse," Hachette and Co., 1898, Paris.

Whishaw, Bernard and Ellen: "Arabic Spain," Smith, Elder and Co., 1912, London.

INDEX